**Viking Trade and Settlement in
Continental Western Europe**

Viking Trade and Settlement in Continental Western Europe

Edited by
Iben Skibsted Klæsøe

Museum Tusculanum Press
University of Copenhagen
2010

Iben Skibsted Klæsøe (ed.): *Viking Trade and Settlement in Continental Western Europe*

© Museum Tusculanum Press and the authors, 2010
Consultant: Ulla Lund Hansen
Copy editors: Christian Falden and Jordy Findanis
Layout, composition and cover design: Pernille Sys Hansen, Damp Design
Printed by Narayana Press, Gylling, www.narayanapress.dk
ISBN 978 87 635 0531 4

Cover illustrations
The Oseberg ship as displayed in Oslo. See p. 32
The Cammin casket. Formerly in the cathedral of Kamień in coastal Pommerania, Poland. Now lost. See p. 150

This book is published with financial support from
Augustinus Fonden
Beckett-Fonden
Carlsbergfondet
Elisabeth Munksgaards Fond
Hielmstierne-Rosencroneske Stiftelse
Konsul George Jorck og Hustru Emma Jorck's Fond
Landsdommer V. Gieses Legat
The Danish Research Council for the Humanities

Museum Tusculanum Press
126 Njalsgade
DK–2300 Copenhagen S
www.mtp.dk

Contents

Iben Skibsted Klæsøe
7 Research history
Some comments

Jan Bill
19 Viking Age ships and seafaring in the West

Egge Knol
43 Frisia in Carolingian times

W.J.H. Verwers
61 Vikings in the lower Rhine area?

Laurent Mazet-Harhoff
81 The incursion of the Vikings into the natural and cultural landscape of upper Normandy

Jens Christian Moesgaard
123 Vikings on the continent
The numismatic evidence

Joël Callais
145 A Thor's hammer found in Normandy

Else Roesdahl
149 Viking art in European churches
(Cammin – Bamberg – Prague – León)

165 Contributors

Iben Skibsted Klæsøe

Research history
Some comments

It is hardly possible to examine the history of research into the Vikings on the Continent without also keeping the Vikings of the insular West in view; these, at least to a certain extent, were clearly the same people who attacked Friesland and France in addition to the British coastline. However, more light seems to have been shed on the Vikings in the British Isles – possibly because, as early as the 17th century, there existed in England considerable interest in their history, literature and language (Wilson 1997: 18). On the other hand, knowledge about the Vikings on the Continent is substantially more limited; in overall terms, very little is known about the Scandinavians who made inroads into the Continental mainland from the end of the 8th to the beginning of the 11th century. Most contemporary accounts are lost and, moreover, some substantial aspects of this period may forever defy clarification. The available knowledge derives largely from written sources compiled by monks (and other literate people) in annals and other texts in Anglo-Saxon and Continental monasteries more than a thousand years ago. But with its historical background and embroidered coloured images, it is also possible to draw upon the Bayeux Tapestry – probably created shortly after the Battle of Hastings in 1066 – as comparative material for the elucidation of the presence of Vikings on the Continent.

Astonishingly, despite the relative abundance of written sources, the corresponding impact of the archaeological remains has only been accorded meagre attention. From an archaeological standpoint, research into Viking activities in the western European part of the Continent has proceeded in a negligent fashion south and west of the Elbe. There are, admittedly, comparatively sparse archaeological remains in this area. The finds consist almost exclusively of stray finds, since closed finds such as graves or hoards are rare.

Contemporary accounts (composed principally in Latin, though some exist in other languages) can only be used with considerable care (Sawyer 1971: 12), particularly since there is uncertainty as to how often a text has been copied. The annals are in themselves a primary source text about the events as they actually happened, or, rather, as to how these were perceived at the time by the authors/scribes concerned. The actual writers of such texts were not historians; neither was it their intention to write history, but rather to leave behind a monument for posterity. Since then it has been the task of the historian to interpret these written sources. Thus it has also been the historians who, in the long course of time, have left their mark on the tradition of the chronicling of research. Meanwhile, however, the significant sources themselves are also available to anybody in easily accessible form (Rau 1955, 1958, 1969; also Albrechtsen in excerpts 1981).

The interest in Vikings, Normans and Danes ebbed and flowed in time with the alternation of cultural focal points within poetry, painting and sculpture (compare illustrations in Mjöberg 1980 and Wilson 1997) in which, respectively, the Romantic mood of the various periods and regions was emphasised – in the same way as the heroic and nationalistic attitudes.

In the catalogue about Vikings and Gods in European art (*Vikinger og Guder i Europæisk Kunst*) accompanying the 1997 exhibition at the Moesgård Museum in Århus, the "History of the Vikings" (Wilson 1997: 7) during the last 400 years was outlined, not only in their native Scandinavia, but also in the territories they conquered. However, it was not until the end of the 12th century or the start of the 13th century that the actual history of the Vikings in the exploits of the Danes (*Gesta Danorum*) was first written down by the Danish chronicler Saxo Grammaticus – taking as his point of departure the narratives and tales of the Norse Sagas. And it was the 19th century which saw the emergence of the first fully collated exegeses of the history of the Vikings, and the inroads they made into Europe, on the basis of the written accounts which were by then one thousand years old.

The current picture is familiar to everybody: heathen hordes from the North in their awe-inspiring – not to say terrifying – ships, pouring ashore along the coasts and rivers of Europe. Through pillage and arson, and by means of military surprise tactics, these quite obviously fearless pirates spread panic and terror among the defenceless Christians throughout almost the entire Occident. It is this very familiar notion which found expression in the literature and art of the 19th – and also in the greater part of the 20th – century, and is totally characteristic not only for England and France, but also for Scandinavia itself. It is only recently that a change in

Iben Skibsted Klæsøe

this perception has come about; this scare-mongering picture of the Vikings, created by literature, began to be challenged and people started to examine the reasons for its emergence.

The four-volume work *Normannerne* ("The Normans") by Johannes Steenstrup from the 19th century (1876–1882), in which he disproves the written sources and previously published literature, is today a classic in that it represents one of the first comprehensive descriptions of the Norsemen and their military ventures in the West. Steenstrup's intention was, among other things, to demonstrate on the basis of the written sources that the "Norsemen [had not abandoned] their Norse customs in the new environment" (Steenstrup 1876, Vol. 1, v) as rapidly as had been suggested by other authors. Against the background of this pioneering work there emerged numerous studies, among which W. Vogel's book *Die Normannen und das fränkische Reich* ("The Normans and the Frankish Realm") must be given prominence. It was published in 1906 and described the period from 799 to 911. Just like Steenstrup, Vogel accepted the information given in the annals and, correspondingly, he narrowed his focus down to the exploits and events which are mentioned in the diverse source material. Subsequent works of history have drawn considerable benefit from the map drawn up by Vogel of the Frankish Kingdom, which incorporates a substantial proportion of the places, rivers, frontiers and Norse remains mentioned in contemporary accounts. Together with the map detailing Viking migrations in the book *The Vikings in Western Christendom* by C.F. Keary from 1891, it formed the basis for later maps of Viking ventures (e.g. Arbman 1961, fig. 15; Arbman 1974, 68; Graham-Campbell 1994, 145). Keary concentrated on the period between 789 and 888 and his momentous book (the exegeses of which are likewise based on the historical sources and the information in the Sagas) ends with the late attack on Paris (885–886) and the "turning point" for the heathen Vikings and their influence on Christian Europe (Keary 1891: 442).

Roughly contemporary with the appearance of these books, a number of archaeological finds came to light in France and Germany which seem to confirm both directly and indirectly the written information concerning the presence of the Vikings on the Continental mainland. Initially such finds were only mentioned in the journals of local museums. However, important attempts were already being made to link the archaeological finds with information about the events of the 9th and 10th centuries. Already in 1865 an

Research history. Some comments

inhumation grave had been discovered in Pîtres near Rouen with two oval brooches from the Viking period (Abbé Cochet 1871), though it was not until 1968 that these finds were acknowledged by a broader consensus of experts (Elmqvist 1969). In 1883 a "double" hoard of treasure was unearthed near Klein-Roscharden in Northwest Germany, which, judging from the coins it included, had been buried around 1005 to 1010. Among the individual finds was a so-called Terslev fibula (Johansen 1912) of Scandinavian origin. The treasure may have been concealed to protect it from a late Viking raid, although previously it was not considered as being part of the accepted picture of the Vikings on the Continent. It was not until 1951 that both these coins (Berghaus 1951) as well as other material (Gandert 1951) were presented to the public.

In 1906 a burial mound on the Île de Groix off the south coast of Brittany was excavated by P. du Chatellier and L. Le Pontois and found to contain the remains of a ship and two people (du Chatellier and Le Pontois 1908). The accompanying weapons were Scandinavian and this type of ship burial also had a Nordic affinity. However, not until 1978 was this ship burial published in modern source-critical terms (Müller-Wille 1978). The find was reported in the first edition of *Das Reallexikon der Germanischen Altertumskunde* (1918–1919), though here it was given only a brief mention. The article dealing with the Vikings, which was written by the Norwegian historian A. Bugge, occupies 22 pages of the lexicon, and deals overwhelmingly with the information from the written sources, while the entire archaeological section (featuring coins, rune stones and individual finds, and information as to how the said items were treated) amounts to no more than two pages.

As early as the first decade of the 20th century, the mention in the literature of a number of isolated, unique works of art in Europe which could be attributed to the Viking period prompted some very interesting conclusions concerning the Scandinavian peoples on the Continent. However knowledge of many of these objects failed to reach a larger, specialist audience since only a few were published in recognised periodicals or publication series. This was the case with both the chests ornamented in the Mammen style from Bamberg and Cammin (Goldschmidt 1918 and 1926; compare also Muhl 1990) and also the magnificent Viking sword from Prague (Paulsen 1933). A further example is the upper part of what is

Iben Skibsted Klæsøe

presumably a censer ornamented in the Jelling style (Paulsen 1932), and a horn from Maastricht, which has secondary ornamentation in the form of pressed fittings in the Mammen style (Hougen 1939; Roes 1940). These are only given sporadic mention, and they too were denied a place in the discussion of Viking influence on the Continent (e.g. Musset 1992).

An initial overview of the sparse material traces found on the western European Continent was finally presented in 1935 by H. Arbman (Arbman & Stenberger 1935: 137–189). Bjørn and Shetelig's great source-work Viking Antiquities in Great Britain and Ireland (Bjørn & Shetelig 1940: 101–131) was somewhat more substantial in content. However, it is by no means exhaustive since it only includes a brief, regional supplementary listing of finds from the Continent complementing the British and Irish finds, and the historical background of these continental finds is not discussed either. Both works are based exclusively on a few chosen visits to museums where, obviously, the only objects cited were those in the public exhibition. The work of the spear head from Termonde in Belgium (*Der Spitze von Termonde*) was the subject of an exhaustive study as early as 1937 (Paulsen 1937).

In the successor to his overview from 1935, H. Arbman, together with his students in Lund, set about an intense study of the archaeological finds from the Seine Region; in this way, not only what was then known as "The Woman's Grave of Pîitres" (Elmqvist 1969) was dealt with, but also a number of weapons (Arbman & Nilsson, 1935). Furthermore this led, perhaps most significantly, to mention of such objects as swords in the specialist literature. This was also the case with a beautifully ornamented Viking-age sword which was discovered in 1929 on the Île de Bièce off the coast of Brittany (Durville 1929). In this context, the connection with the migration of the Vikings both south of Brittany and in the Loire Valley, together with the short-term settlement at Nantes, were discussed. At both Buxtehude and Hamburg (Jankuhn 1950–51; Müller-Wille 1970) swords were likewise unearthed which were associated with the conflicts in the North German territories between the Carolingians and the Vikings, including the 845 attack on the Hammaburg. Early medieval swords were also discovered in several locations in the Netherlands – principally in rivers – and published (Braat 1960; Ypey 1960–61, 1962–63), their presence having been interpreted as due to the periods of unrest between the Carolingians and the Vikings. Since 1978 all discoveries on the western European Continent of swords regarded as Viking have undergone critical examination, only about a dozen

Research history. Some comments

examples have passed as original (Müller-Wille 1978: 70–74). Similarly sobering, a critical evaluation of what had previously been regarded as Viking finds from the Netherlands, had shown these discoveries to be actually severely limited in number (van Regteren Altena and Heidinga 1977). In any case, neither of the last two examples is based on a complete collation of data of the storerooms, and thus, in spite of everything, they can only be considered summary appraisals.

In the first half of the 20th century repeated examples of correspondence were seen between the archaeological material and the written historical sources. However, by the end of the 1960s the characteristic mode of presentation, depending almost solely on the written sources, began to change. Gradually the archaeological evidence was increasingly drawn upon in the representation of the Vikings on the Continent (Brøndsted 1960: 95 ff.; Arbman 1961: 82 f.); the English historian P. Sawyer argued in its favour that the archaeological testimony could support the historical sources (Sawyer 1971: 123) – though the reverse was apparently not possible.

In various Dutch publications, Friesland is often awarded great attention in a Viking context. According to the written sources, Friesland is one of those areas which was almost continually at the mercy of Viking attacks in the period 810–1010 (Besteman 1999: 253). However, there is little archaeological evidence for this, apart from sporadic individual finds (van Heeringen 1990a and 1990b), principally from Dorestad (Roes 1965; Verwers 1998) and also Domburg (Capelle 1976). Most recently discovered is the spectacular hoard of silver from Westerklief (Besteman 1997 and 1999), which has decidedly broadened our knowledge of Vikings on the Continent. This information has been supplemented through the investigation of the marketplace at Dorestad (and its surroundings) in the Netherlands (Holwerde 1930; van Es & Verwers 1980; Verwers 1998), which was one of the most important Carolingian marketplaces and, according to the contemporary sources, was subject to repeated Viking attacks and pillage from 830.

Nevertheless, the attempt to see concordance between archaeological and historical (i.e. textual) testimony has also led to a situation in which a number of objects have reached museums over the course of time whose authenticity is not uncontested. The most famous of these is without doubt the so-called Winsum Treasure (Boeles 1951) which has been re-

Iben Skibsted Klæsøe

garded unequivocally as a forgery since 1975 (Elzinga 1975). Not only in the Netherlands, but also in Belgium are there a number of "Viking finds" which have either been recognised as fakes, or had previously been incorrectly classified, or rather had shown themselves to be French at the earliest (van Regteren Altena & Heidinga 1977).

In regional terms it is, however, Normandy which has attracted the greatest attention from scholars. The Bayeux Tapestry, with its representation of the political relations between England and Normandy around 1066 which left their mark on various names in the area (Stenton 1957; Wilson 1985), has naturally promoted an increased awareness of Vikings in Normandy. Nevertheless, it is particularly the region's "Norse-sounding" names – above all place names – which have attracted the attention of scholars. The linguistic heritage, such as –thorp, –dalle and hoguen, or a name such as Auberville (which means Asbjörndorf in German) (Musset 1992: 93), is indicative of Viking presence in that area. Research into place names was of crucial significance for the French historian and linguist, M. Lucien Musset, who as early as 1942 published his first major work concerning the Viking influence in Normandy, and has subsequently produced numerous publications on the Vikings (i.a. Musset 1992). Proceeding from his many years of research into names, he concluded that many Vikings in Normandy were of Anglo-Saxon extraction (Nissen Jaubert, forthcoming). The research into place names is one of those fields important for other scholars (Fellows-Jensen 1988; Gautier 1954; Marechal 1959). Through the incorporation of this research we have arrived at a more reliable image of the Vikings, both in England and on the Continental mainland, which has predominated since 1970 and has also already been reflected in *The Vikings in Francia* (Wallace-Hadrill 1975).

For the Belgian historian A. D'Haenens, who has written on both the Vikings in Belgium (1967) and in Normandy (1970), the point of departure is "That we know less than we thought we knew…" (cf. Wallace-Hadrill 1975: 4, note 12). In *Les invasions Normandes, une catastrophe?* (1970), D'Haenens, working from the data provided by the contemporary sources, takes a deliberate stand against the negative perception of the Viking campaigns, which, in the West, were essentially undertaken by the Danes. It is D'Haenens' opinion that the Viking raids occasioned significantly less destruction than was usually supposed, and that a positive effect should instead be recognised, which in the course of time led to integration. A recent

Research history. Some comments

historian of wider significance is H. Zettel, who, in *Das Bild der Normannen und Normanneneinfälle in westfränkischen, ostfränkischen und angelsächsischen Quellen des 8. bis 11. Jahrhunderts* (1977), offers an impressive and painstaking presentation and exegesis of the historical accounts. One of the areas he explores is the development of research with regard to the political and cultural understanding of the Vikings, but he also deals with the motivation behind their ventures, their fighting technique and the wide-spread concept of Danelaw.

However, in the last 30 years research has also been dominated by themes tackled in an interdisciplinary fashion. Now it is no longer solely the historians who are the exclusive contributors to the greater knowledge of the Vikings on the Continent. In this way, a multifaceted image emerges of the peoples from the North and their influence. In addition to name research, numismatics is also an important field from which much has been drawn in recent times (Dumas 1979). Then there are the ships which are mentioned hundreds of times in the written sources: much consideration has been given to them and the routes they sailed (Crumlin-Pedersen 1997; Ellmers 1972 and 1966). Supplementary to this are a number of contemporary depictions from the Continent of Viking ships (Capelle 1998): the Bayeux Tapestry, in fact, displays an entire fleet, including a royal vessel with a banner and bearing a cross blessed by the Pope.

The political and commercial aspects have been dealt with in a number of publications, e.g. in *Kings and Vikings* from 1984 written by P. Sawyer. This work also brings into the Viking context the Continental ring of forts along the mainland coast, some remains of which are still identifiable in rural areas bordering the shore. New excavations, of paramount importance being those undertaken at Middelbourg on Walcheren, hark back to the earliest traces of settlement at the beginning of the 9th century (van Heeringen et al. 1995). The data concerning the Viking hordes and their actual magnitude have been dealt with by a number of scholars. However *The Viking Art of War* by P. Griffith (1995) provides the first overview worth discussion of Viking military strategy seen from the perspective of modern military analysis. Taking as her points of departure coins and forts, the English scholar J. Nelson has produced a special exposition of the political history of the period (Nelson 1988). In one of her works (Nelson 1988) she arrives at the conclusion that, "the Continental evidence shows not the legen-

Iben Skibsted Klæsøe

dary Viking faces of committed rapists and murderers..." (Nelson 1988: 19). Finally, mention must be made of several other works presenting surveys (Roesdahl 1987 and 1992; Graham-Campbell 1997; Nelson 1997); however, when seeking to illustrate their points these authors have done no more than fall back on previously known archaeological material.

Seen in international terms, there is a fundamental difference in research dealing with the Vikings. While in the North the Viking period belongs to prehistory, outside Scandinavia the period is reckoned to be part of the Middle Ages. Factors such as which individuals and disciplines have been concerned with the field have naturally also exerted an influence. In France, however, even when the opportunities for making outright statements or declarations are limited, it is regarded as necessary to continue undertaking increased archaeological investigations (Périn 1990 and Marin 1997). This also applies in the case of the Netherlands following the discovery of the Westerklief Treasure (Besteman 1999).

What is still lacking, however, is a complete register of all the finds which can stand in context together with the presence, so well documented in writing, of the Vikings in western Europe. At this stage, only when this systematic inventory is put forward, will a well-balanced evaluation of events, supplemented also by the archaeological perspective, be possible.

Note

I would like to express my gratitude and warm thanks to Prof., Dr. Habil. Torsten Capelle, who has been of great help to me and in cooperation with whom this chapter was written.

Translated from German by Neil Stanford

References

Albrechtsen, E., *Vikingerne i Franken*. Second impression (Odense 1981).

Arbman, H., *The Vikings* (London 1961).

Arbman, H. & M. Stenberger, *Vikingar i västerled* (Stockholm 1935).

Arbman, H. & N.-O. Nilsson, "Armes Scandinaves de L'Époque Viking en France". *Meddelanden från Lunds Universitets Historiska Museum 1966/68* (Lund 1969), pp. 163–202.

Berghaus, P., "Die Münzen von Klein-Roscharden". *Oldenburger Jahrbuch* 51 (1951), pp. 196–206.

Besteman, J.C., "De vondst van Westerklief, gemeente Wieringen: Én Zilverschat uit de Vikingperiode". *Oudheidkundige Mededelingen uit het Rijksmuseum van Oudheden te Leiden* 77 (1997), pp. 199–226.

— "Viking Silver on Wieringen. A Viking Age Silver Hoard from Westerklief on the Former Isle of Wieringen (Province of North Holland) in the Light of the Viking Relations with Frisia". In: H. Sarfatij, W.J.H. Verwers & P.J. Woltering (eds), *In Discussion with the Past. Archaeological Studies Presented to W.A. van Es* (Amersfoort 1999), pp. 253–266.

Bjørn, A. & H. Shetelig, *Viking Antiquities in Great Britain and Ireland* IV (Oslo 1940).

Boeles, P.C.J.A., *Friesland tot de elfde eeuv. Zijn vöör- en vroege geschiedenis* (Gravenhage 1951).

Braat, W.C., "Acht frühmittelalterliche Schwerter aus dem Rijksmuseum van Oudheden zu Leiden". *Analecta Archaeologica. Festschrift Fritz Fremersdorf* (Cologne 1960), pp. 53–56.

Brøndsted, J., *Vikingerne* (Copenhagen 1960).

Bugge, A. Wikinger, *Reallexikon der Germanischen Altertumskunde* vol. 4. Gen. ed. Johannes Hoops (Strasbourg 1918–1919), pp. 529–553.

Capelle, T., *Die frühgeschichtlichen Metallfunde von Domburg auf Walcheren* 1–2. Nederlandse Oudheden. Rijksdienst voor het Oudheidkundig Bodemonderzoek. ROB. 5 (Amersfoort 1976).

Capelle, T., "Nicht nur Nacht- und Nebelaktionen". In: U. Löber (ed.), *Die Wikinger*. Landesmuseum Koblenz (Koblenz 1998), pp. 87–94.

Chatellier, P. du & L. Le Pontois, "La sépulture scandinave à barque de l'Île de Groix". *Bulletin de la Societé Archéologique du Finistère* 35 (1908), pp. 3–98.

Cochet, M. Abbé, "Notice sur Deux Fibules Scandinaves Trouvées à Pitres (Eure) en 1865 et Entrées au Musee de Rouen". *Extrait du Précis de l'Académie de Rouen pour l'année 1869-1870* (Rouen 1871), pp. 408–420.

Crumlin-Petersen, O., *Viking-Age Ships and Shipbuildings in Hedeby/Haithabu and Schleswig* (Schleswig and Roskilde 1997).

D'Haenens, A., *Les Invasions normands en Belgique au IXe Siècle* (Louvai 1967).

— *Les invasions Normandes, une catastrophe?* (Paris 1970).

Dumas, F., "Les Monnairees normandes". *Revue Numismatique* 6.21 (1979), pp. 84–140.

Durville, G., "Les épées Normandes de l'Ile de Bièce". *Bulletin de la société Archéologique et Historique de Nantes et de la Loire-Inférieure. Fondée le 9 aout 1845* (Nantes 1929), pp. 121–146.

Ellmers, D., "Frühmittelalterliche Handelsschiffahrt in Mittel- und Nordeuropa". *Offa-Bücher* 28 (Neumünster 1972).

Elmqvist, B., "Les fibules de Pîtres". *Meddelanden från Lunds Universitets Historiska Museum* (Lund 1969), pp. 203–224.

Elzinga, G. Rondom de, "Vikingsschat van Winsum". *De Vrije Fries* (1975), pp. 82–122.

Es, W.A. van & W.H.J. Verwers, *Excavations at Dorestad 1. The Habour: Hoogstraat 1*. Nederlandse Oudheden 9. Kromme Rijn Projekt 1. ROB (Amersfoort 1980).

Fellows-Jensen, G., "Scandinavian place-names and Viking settlement in Normandy: A review". *Namn och Bygd* 76 (1988), pp. 113–137.

Gandert, O.-F., "Die Oldenburgischen Silberschatzfunde von Klein-Roschaden (Kreiss Cloppenburg)". *Oldenburger Jahrbuch* 51 (1951), pp. 151–195.

Goldschmidt. M., *Die Elfenbeinskulpturen II aus der Zeit der karolingischen und sächsischen Kaiser VIII.–XI. Jahrhundert* (Berlin 1918).

— *Die Elfenbeinskulpturen* IV (Berlin 1926).

Graham-Campbell, J. (ed.), *Cultural Atlas of the Viking World* (Oxfordshire 1994).

— (ed.), *Die Wikinger – Bildatlas der Weltkulturen* (Augsburg 1997).

Griffith, P., *The Viking Art of War* (London 1995).

Heeringen, R.M. van 1990a. "Én zilveren toiletgarnituur uit de Vikingtijd van het strand van Domburg". *Walacria* 3 (1990), pp. 51–60.

— 1990b. "Én Viking-sieraad van het strand van Callantsoog, Noord-Holland". *Westerheem* 39 (1990), pp. 22–23.

Hougen, B., "Et Anglo-Skandinavisk Drikkehorn i Holland". *Viking* 16 (Oslo 1939), pp. 115–128.

Jankuhn, H., "Schwerter des frühen Mittelalters aus Hamburg". *Hammaburg* 2. 1950/51 (Hamburg 1951), pp. 31–37.

Johansen, K. Friis, "Sølvskatten fra Terslev".

Iben Skibsted Klæsøe

Aarbøger for nordisk Oldkyndighed og Historie (Copenhagen 1912).

Keary, C.F., *The Vikings in Western Christendom* (London 1891).

Marechal, J.M., "Causes et effets de æ'esprit colonisateur des Scandinaves". *Annales de Normandie* 4 (1959), pp. 257–272.

Marin, J.-Y., "Les Vikings à la conquête de la Normandie". *L'Historie* 207 (1997), pp. 50–57.

Mjöberg, J., "Romanticism and Revival. The Northern Wold". In: D.M. Wilson (ed.), *The History and Heritage of Northern Europe AD 400-1000* (New York 1980), pp. 207–238.

Muhl, A., "Der Bamberger und der Camminer Schrein. Zwei im Mammenstil verzierte Prunkkästchhen der Wikingerzeit". *Offa* 47 (1990).

Musset, L., "Skandinaverne og det vesteuropeiske kontinent". In: E. Roesdahl (ed.), *Viking og Hvidekrist. Norden og Europa 800-1200* (Copenhagen 1992), pp. 88–95.

Müller-Wille, "M. Ein neues ULFBERHT-Schwert aus Hamburg". *Offa* 27 (1970), pp. 65–88.

— "M. Das Schiffsgrab von der Île de Groix (Bretagne) – Ein Exkurs zum 'Bootkammergrab von Haithabu'". *Berichte über die Ausgrabungen in Haithabu* 12 (1978), pp. 48–84.

Nelson, J., "The Vikings on the Continent". *History Today* 38 (1988), pp. 12–19.

— "The Frankish Empire". In: P. Sawyer (ed.), *The Oxford Illustrated History of the Vikings* (Oxford 1997), pp. 19–47.

Paulsen, B., "Ein Altargerät aus der Wikingerzeit". *Acta Archaeologica*, vol. III (Copenhagen 1932).

— "Wikingerfunde aus Ungarn im Lichte der nord- und westeuropäischen Frühgeschichte". *Archaeologis Hungarica* XII (Budapest 1933).

— "Die Wikingerlanze von Termonde in Belgien. Manus". *Zeitschrift für Deutsche Vorgeschichte*, vol. 33 (Leipzig 1937), pp. 381–411.

Périn, P., "Les Objects Vikings du Musée des Antiquités de la Seine-Maritime, A Rouen". *Recueil d'études en hommage à Lucien Musset. Cahier des Annales de Normandie* 23 (Caen 1990), pp. 161–188.

Rau, R. (ed.), *Quellen zur karolingischen Reichsgeschichte I-III*. Ausgewählte quellen zur deutschen Geschichte des Mittelalters V-VII (Darmstadt 1955, 1958, 1969).

Regteren Altena, J.F. van & H.A. Heidinga, "The North Sea Region in the Early Medieval Period (400-950)". In: *EX HORREO (Festschrift für W. Glasbergen)* (Amsterdam 1977), pp. 47–67.

Roes, A., "Drinking Horn of the Viking Period". *Mededeelingen der Koninklijke Nederlandsche Akademie van Wetenschappen, Afd. Letterkunde. Nieuwe Reeks*, vol. 3. no. 3 (Amsterdam 1940).

— "Vondsten van Dorestad". *Archaeologica Traiectina* 7 (Groningen 1965).

Roesdahl, E., *Vikingernes Verden* (Copenhagen 1987).

— (ed.), *Viking og Hvidekrist. Norden og Europa 800-1200* (Copenhagen 1992).

Sawyer, P., *The Age of the Vikings* (London 1971).

— *Kings and Vikings. Scandinavia and Europe AD 700-1100* (London and New York 1984).

Steenstrup, J., *Normannerne*, vols 1–4. 1876–1882 (Copenhagen 1878).

Stenton, F., *Der Wandteppich von Bayeux* (Cologne 1957).

Verwers, W.J.H., "Dorestad und der Handel der Wikinger". In: U. Löber (ed.), *Die Wikinger* (Koblenz 1998), pp. 107–115.

Vogel, W., *Die Normannen und das fränkische Reich bis zur Gründung der Normandie*. Heidelberger Abhandlungen zur mittleren und neueren Geschichte 14 (Heidelberg 1906).

Wallace-Hadrill, J.M., *The Vikings in Francia. The Stenton Lecture 1974* (University of Reading 1975).

Wilson, D.M., *Der Teppich von Bayeux* (Frankfurt and Berlin 1985).

— *Vikinger og Guder i Europæisk Kunst* (Højbjerg 1997).

Ypey, J., "Én aantal vroeg-middeleeuwse zwarden uit Nederlandse musea". *Berichten van de Rijksdienst voor het Oudheidkundig Bodemonderzoek* 10–11 (Amersfoort 1960–61), pp. 368–394.

— "Vroeg-middeleeuwse wapens uit Nederlandse versamelingen". *Berichten van de Rijksdienst voor het Oudheidkundig Bodemonderzoek* 12–13 (Amersfoort 1962–63), pp. 153–176.

Zettel, H., *Das Bild der Normannen und der Normanneneinfälle in westfränkischen, ostfränkischen und angelsächsischen Quellen des 8. bis 11. Jahrhunderts* (Munich 1977).

Jan Bill

Viking Age ships and seafaring in the West

Introduction

The geography of Scandinavia has always made seafaring an indispensable tool to its population.[1] The interior of the Scandinavian Peninsula is covered with deep forests and mountains, so human habitation occurred mostly along its coasts, lakes and rivers. The waterways were also the routes along which communication and trade could most easily take place, and the key role of ships and seafaring is reflected in the frequent use of the ship in religious iconography and as a display of power and wealth throughout Scandinavian prehistory.[2]

In the Viking Age the entire northern part of Europe was interconnected by seafaring that rapidly developed its capacity for transporting people and goods to levels unprecedented since Roman times. The Scandinavians were only one of the many agents in this development; but compared to the situation in other parts of Northern Europe, an astonishingly large number of Scandinavian Viking Age ships have been found. These finds have contributed to the Scandinavians' achieving in history a role far more dominant in the literature about North European seafaring in the 8th–11th centuries than is justified in reality. The scattered and fragmentary character of the archaeological evidence from Britain, Ireland and the southern coast of the North Sea and the Channel makes it difficult to compare shipbuilding in these regions with that of Scandinavia; but an argument *ex silentio* about the inferior character of shipbuilding in these regions should not be put forward. If anything, the material shows shipbuilding traditions that sometimes differed from, but were as complex as, those of Scandinavia.[3]

The westward expansion of the Scandinavians in the late 8th to 11th centuries was, however, predominantly a maritime enterprise that benefited from the maritime skills of coastal societies in Scandinavia. Ships were key tools in sporadic trade and plunder activities, as well as in organised military expeditions. In the case of colonisation, ships and seafaring constituted communication lines of crucial importance for the new Scandinavian settlements. Some settlements, like those in Ireland, Normandy and the Danelaw, were soon to abandon their political ties with Scandinavia, while others – first and foremost the island societies of the North Atlantic – remained closely connected with Denmark and Norway for centuries.

Knowledge about Scandinavian shipbuilding and seafaring is therefore of significant importance, not only for the understanding of the Scandinavian Viking Age expansion but also for obtaining an impression of the general character of seafaring in Northern Europe at that time. The aim of this article is to provide such information for researchers working with other aspects of Scandinavian influences in the West, and also to discuss some currently unresolved questions about early Viking Age seafaring that are of specific relevance in this context. This discussion will focus especially on the date for the introduction of the sail to Scandinavian shipbuilding, and on the extent to which our only significant ship-find from this period, the Oseberg ship, can be regarded as representative of early 9th-century seafaring.[4] At the end of the paper, a short discussion will try to estimate how many men Viking fleets may have carried – a question relevant to the ongoing discussion about the size of early medieval armies.[5]

The source material

Ship-finds – in this paper defined as finds of vessels more than 12 metres long – from the Viking Age and preceding centuries are a small and only slowly increasing body. In Scandinavia, the number of 8th–10th-century ship-finds is well below 50, and if we include only those that can and have been reconstructed with some certainty, they total little more than a dozen. Even more limited is the material from Western Europe, from where only two such finds have been published thus far. However, a few new wreck-finds and a growing number of finds of reused ship timbers, paired with the experiences gained from experimental ship archaeology and the improved dating of ship-finds owing to the developing discipline of dendrochronology, have led to significant progress being made in research into Viking Age seafaring in the last several years.

The first excavation that actually made possible the tentative reconstruction of a Scandinavian vessel of the Viking Age took place at Tune in Norway in 1867.[6] Since then a total of 14 more excavations have been carried out in Scandinavia, fig. 1. Four of the five oldest finds – from Tune, Gokstad and Oseberg in Norway and from Ladby in Denmark – are all

	Dating (AD)	Length (metres)	Oars	Capacity (tons or men)	Provenance (dendrochr.)	Context	Reference
Finds in W. Scandinavia							
Kvalsund 2	c. 700	18				Sacrifice	H. Shetelig and F. Johannessen, 1929
Oseberg	820	21.5				Grave	A.W. Brøgger et al., 1917
Gokstad	895-900	23.2			Norway	Grave	A.W. Brøgger and H. Shetelig, 1951
Tune	c. 910	20			Norway	Grave	A.W. Brøgger and H. Shetelig, 1951
Ladby	900-950	21.5				Grave	K. Thorvildsen, 1957
Hedeby 1	c. 985	30.9	58		Denmark	Wreck	O. Crumlin-Pedersen, 1997a
Klåstad	c. 990	21				Wreck	A.E. Christensen and G. Leiro, 1976
Äskekärr 1	c. 1000	15.8				Wreck	A. Bråthen, 1998; P. Humbla, 1934
Hedeby 3	1025	c. 22			Denmark	Wreck	O. Crumlin-Pedersen, 1997a
Skuldelev 1	1030-1050	16.3			W. Norway	Barrier	O. Olsen and O. Crumlin-Pedersen, 1968
Skuldelev 2	1042-1043	c. 30			Ireland	Barrier	O. Olsen and O. Crumlin-Pedersen, 1968
Skuldelev 3	1030-1050	14			Denmark	Barrier	O. Olsen and O. Crumlin-Pedersen, 1968
Skuldelev 5	1030-1050	17.5			Denmark	Barrier	O. Olsen and O. Crumlin-Pedersen, 1968
Roskilde 3	1060	18				Wreck	J. Bill et al., 2000
Roskilde 6	after 1025	c. 36				Wreck	J. Bill, M. Gøthche, and H.M. Myrhøj, 2000
Finds in the West							
Graveney	910-975	c. 14				Wreck	V. Fenwick, 1978
Utrecht	c. 1000	17.2				Wreck	A. van de Moortel, 2000; R. Vlek, 1987

grave-finds originating from princely burials of the 9th or 10th centuries. The oldest one, the Kvalsund 1 boat, was found broken up in a bog, and was probably a sacrifice. On the other hand, later finds have all been from marine locations, where they were either sunk as parts of sea-route barriers, or had been wrecked or abandoned in coastal locations. Thus there exists a marked difference in context between the older and the younger finds that calls for caution when comparing and interpreting the group of finds as a whole.[7]

Fig. 1. Reconstructed ship-finds from Scandinavia and the North Sea area, AD 700–1100.

The chronological and geographical distributions of the finds are uneven. From the period AD 700–950, there is an average of only one find every 50 years, while for the next 150 years there is an average yield of one new ship-find every 15 years. Geographically it can be noted that all the finds of early ships – apart from Ladby – have been made in Norway, while all the younger ones apart from Äskekärr in Western Sweden and the Klåstad find from Norway were excavated in Denmark, more precisely in Roskilde Fjord and in the harbour of Hedeby. However interesting the find places may be, the ships' places of construction have also contributed to our understanding of those examples where it has been possible to establish a provenance: The Gokstad ship and two of the Skuldelev ships appear to derive from Southern and Western Norway respectively, while two other Skuldelev ships and the two from Hedeby are local in origin. One Skuldelev ship, the large longship, is from Dublin. It is noticeable that all the ship-finds derive from Western Scandinavia. So far, the only East Scandinavian find of a purported Viking Age ship is the Lapuri wreck from Finland.[8] This find, however, does show biased dating evidence and deviates in terms of construction significantly from hitherto known Scandinavian finds from the Viking Age, and for these reasons it will not be included in the present context.

Turning to Western Europe, the two finds in question are the 10th-century Graveney Boat from Kent in England and the Utrecht Boat from the Netherlands, recently dated by dendrochronology to the early 11th century.[9] Both these vessels deviate markedly in construction from the Scandinavian ships but partial finds demonstrate that they are representative of centuries-long regional shipbuilding traditions in south-eastern England and the Rhine Delta respectively. Other partial finds, for example from Dublin, show that the Scandinavian settlers to a high degree brought their shipbuilding traditions with them when colonising, and that these traditions prevailed for centuries.[10] However, published archaeological ship-finds from AD 700–1100 from the North Sea and Channel region are still few.

Seafaring in Viking Age Northern Europe

Seafaring in Northern Europe from the 8th to 11th century took place in open vessels and is thought, for longer voyages, to have been more or less restricted to the summer half of the year. From High and Late Medieval written sources, it appears that it was common to have to wait extensive periods for fair weather before starting journeys, and this is probably true for earlier times as well. Well under sail, however, the distances to be covered in Northern Europe are not excessive, and even the widest extensions of open water, like the North Sea, are little more than 600 km wide, and could be crossed within 4–5 days. It is thought that coastal navigation was dominant, but not exclusive for blue-water crossings. Propulsion was provided by a single square sail, sometimes supplemented with oars, and steering by a side-hung rudder. Shipbuilding and seafaring changed significantly during the period, and probably in a pattern involving significant regional differences, between the Baltic and the North Sea region, for example.

The early ships found at Oseberg, Tune and Gokstad are all quite broad vessels that allow for a larger crew than was necessary for handling the oars and/or for a marginal cargo capacity. For the Gokstad ship, for example, a cargo capacity of *c.* 7 tons has been suggested.[11] In terms of early-9th-century trade, this is a respectable cargo volume, and there is hardly

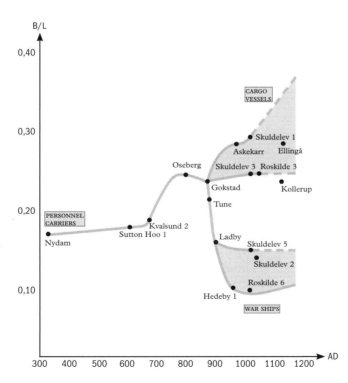

Fig. 2. Variations in the beam/length ratio, after Crumlin-Pedersen 1999, with data added for the preliminary reconstruction of the Tune, Roskilde 3 and Roskilde 6 ships.

Viking Age ships and seafaring in the West

any doubt that in terms of capacity, ships of the Gokstad type would have been able to fulfil the transport needs of Scandinavian involvement in early Viking Age trade, as well as piracy and warfare.

The ship-finds following the Gokstad-Oseberg-Tune group all differ in character from these, as they are all either much more slender personnel carriers, or even broader cargo vessels that were equipped with oars only for restricted manoeuvring purposes. It has been suggested that this evidence represents a specialisation of an earlier, all-round type of vessel.[12] Although the schematic visualisation of this idea in fig. 2 may be somewhat simplistic, it is probably correct to see the 10th century as a phase of transformation for Scandinavian seafaring, with the introduction of specialised cargo carriers as the most important sign that a new type of society was gaining ground. The development in cargo capacity in this period gives a good impression of the impact of this change; for example, the mere 7 tons of the Gokstad ship around AD 900 changes to the *c.* 60 tons of the Hedeby 3 ship around AD 1025. This additional capacity provided the necessary cargo capacity for bulk trade, but it also made it possible to maintain, on a regular basis, the contacts to the remote settlements in the North Atlantic from where important resources were obtained. The earliest of the specialised cargo carriers are the Klåstad ship, dated by dendrochronology to *c.* AD 990, and the Äskekärr ship, with a somewhat disputed, dendrochronological date of the early 11th century.[13]

The development of the personnel carriers is no less astonishing. As they increased in length, there was an increase in the number of men carried, even though they were built more slender than before. For the longest longships – the Skuldelev 2, Hedeby 1 and Roskilde 6 – the estimated number of oars varies between 58–68, and the total crew size between 60–100. The specialisation gave some other advantages, especially in terms of speed and manoeuvrability, but perhaps also made it possible to use bows and spears more efficiently in the initial missile exchange that preceded boarding, the ultimate goal of sea battles at that time. Still, the primary role of the longships was to serve as personnel transporters rather than as fighting platforms. From an economic point of view, the remarkable change is that it became possible – and expedient – to build ships that exclusively served military purposes. The late Viking Age longships had extremely limited cargo capacities, and were dependent on their large crews for maintaining stability. Only in extremely prestige-oriented trade systems would they

Jan Bill

have been able to play a role in trade. The development of the specialised longships in the 10th and 11th centuries thus represents the existence of a society that was sufficiently rich and organised to make investments in ships that could be used for nothing but warfare and in displays of power.

Turning to the west, the almost complete absence of finds that are sufficiently well-preserved to allow reconstruction makes it impossible to draw close parallels to the Scandinavian development. The Graveney boat, probably abandoned around AD 950, is a small cargo carrier that had been used for local transport in the Thames estuary and possibly for cross-Channel voyages. It was built in a specific style that is documented as having found widespread use in Anglo-Saxon England and thus demonstrates the presence of specialised cargo carriers in this area in the 10th century.[14] Finds of ship fragments in London demonstrate that large ships, comparable to the Hedeby 3 cargo ship, did call at the harbour in pre-conquest London, although the origin of these vessels is not known.[15]

The introduction of the sail

The question about the character of seafaring in Northern and Western Europe at the beginning of the Viking Age is a matter of some dispute. A long-held, but not very soundly based, view is that no seafaring of significance existed between the collapse of the Western Roman Empire and the Viking Age and that this was in part the reason for the success of the Scandinavian pirates of the 8th and 9th centuries: their counterparts had no naval traditions and therefore easily fell prey to the sea-borne attackers. This viewpoint has been questioned during the last few decades, especially by the suggestion of direct, pre-Viking connections across the North Sea.[16]

Primarily on the basis of documentary evidence, the British historian John Haywood in his book from 1991 demonstrates that piratical and naval activities were anything but rare among Franks, Saxons, and Frisians during the 3rd to 7th centuries.[17] He even makes a case for the continuous use of the sail in the North Sea, a theory that has otherwise been rejected owing to the lack of archaeological evidence between the collapse of the Western Roman Empire and the eve of the Viking Age. Although Haywood confines himself to working with written sources concerning the Franks, Saxons and Frisians, he does include Scandinavian finds in his discussion of the archaeological evidence. His work can therefore be read, and has been, as a testi-

Fig. 3. The Karlby stone, a stray find from Djursland, Jutland. The stone measures 22 mm across. Photo: The Viking Ship Museum, Roskilde.

mony to the early introduction of sail also in Scandinavian shipbuilding.[18] Haywood refers to the Karlby stone from eastern Jutland, which, in spite of its small proportions, clearly shows a sailing ship with a side rudder, fig. 3. Haywood argues that owing to its similarity with the 4th-century Nydam boat – in which no signs of rigging have been found – the picture on the Karlby stone has to be taken as an indication of the use of sail in the 4th century.[19] The Karlby stone, however, is a stray find, and its date is therefore based on stylistic, rather than scientific, methods.[20] Other researchers stress the similarity of the Karlby-stone ship's hull shape to that of the Sutton Hoo ship and thus suggest a 7th-century date for the only 12 mm long engraving, but further possibilities can also be mentioned.[21] The character of the sail and the indications of animal heads on the stem and stern are reminiscent of Gotland picture stones from the 7th–9th centuries, or of images on some Dorestad and Hedeby coins. Both the ship and the deer on the reverse of the Karlby stone are popular early Viking Age motives that can be found in many places, for example in the official iconography and graffiti of the Oseberg find from the first half of the 9th century.[22] Taking the size of the stone and the motives into consideration, combined with the observation that they do not seem to have been made within any known artistic style or with any specific known artistic purpose, it is hardly possible to date the ship depiction any more closely than to a period when both the side rudder and the square sail were in use – which of course does not help us to date the introduction of sail into Scandinavian shipbuilding.

Jan Bill

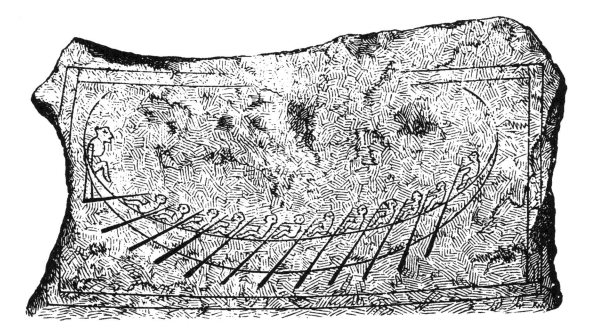

Fig. 4. The Häggeby stone from *c.* 500, Uppland, Sweden, is one of the few finds of picture stones made in mainland Sweden. The characteristics of the vessel are similar to those of the contemporary Gotland ship depictions. Length 1.62 m. After O. Montelius, 1910, Taf. 34B.

Secure evidence for the use of sail in Scandinavia occurs late. Picture stones from Eastern Sweden and Gotland continue to display rowed vessels throughout the 5th and 6th centuries, documenting that oars were, if not the only mode of propulsion, then at least that which was associated with status, fig. 4. Sailing ships first appear on the Gotland picture stones in the 7th and 8th centuries, or perhaps even a century later, if a suggested revision of their dating is accepted.[23] Comparable finds do not exist in Western Scandinavia, where the presence of sail is not attested until the Oseberg ship from AD 820. The advanced rigging of the Oseberg ship attests, however, that its shipbuilders already possessed extensive experience concerning the constructional aspects of building sailing ships. It is of interest that still in the late 7th century, two finds demonstrate that large rowing vessels without sails were almost certainly being built in Norway. The Kvalsund 1 boat

Viking Age ships and seafaring in the West

from around AD 700 is 18 m long and 3 m wide.[24] The boat carried 20 oarsmen and had room for some additional crew-members. It was, as already mentioned, sacrificed, and had been violently destroyed at the time of deposition, which leaves some uncertainty concerning its original construction. The other example is a vessel at least 19 metres long used as a grave ship in the Storhaug mound on Karmøy. Recent 14C analyses combined with studies of the artefacts from the grave date this burial between AD 680–750. The documentation of the ship-find, excavated in 1886, is inconsistent, but because of the absence of any signs of a keelson or mast partner, or other indications of rigging, it is believed that the ship was constructed for rowing only.[25]

It thus appears that the rowing ship was still connected with the dominant class in Scandinavian society by the 7th century. This does not exclude the possibility of sails being known and used, but there is no evidence, at present, that sailing ships played any significant role. It may seem paradoxical that a relatively simple technology like the sail had for centuries not been introduced in a maritime-oriented society like Scandinavia, when it was seemingly being used in neighbouring areas. However, this may not be quite as incredible as it sounds, for several reasons. Firstly, most of the evidence that Haywood presents as arguments for the Germanic use of sail merely attests to the impressive range of their piratical activities – only one source, from AD 473, directly mentions Saxon use of sail.[26] It is not clear, however, whether this source refers to Saxons coming from the British Isles, or from the Continent. Other references are circumstantial and, in my opinion, highly dubious, such as Haywood's mention of a 4th-century text that compares the Saxons to desert raiders on the eastern frontier of the Empire, who "appear where the wind guides them", and takes this to suggest that the Saxons used sails.[27] The evidence for widespread use of sail among the Germanic tribes in the North Sea area is not very strong, and does not allow us to conclude that this was the dominant mode of propulsion.

Secondly, the knowledge of a certain technology does not automatically lead to its adoption in society; in order to be accepted, a technology has to be considered useful, and not a threat to social stability. While it is hard to imagine that anyone should not find it more useful to be transported by a swelling sail rather than sweating over oars, the social aspect may be of importance. In maritime societies like the Scandinavian ones, ships formed an important part of the power structure, and the religious and

Jan Bill

symbolic role of ships is well attested.[28] A radical change of communication technology, such as changing from rowing to sailing ships, would inevitably revolutionise a sea-dependent society. It is also to be noted that the southern North Sea coast and the Channel area were much closer to the demographic, economic and political centre of Western Europe than Scandinavia. This may well help to explain why sails were being used in these areas, and not further to the northeast. A final factor also to be taken into consideration is the barrier effect of the west coast of Jutland. The southern North Sea coast, from Blåvandshuk in the north to the old Rhine mouth in the south, was at that time an area with very different conditions for seafaring than the west coast of Jutland, and the latter may have presented Frisian and Saxon shipbuilders with problems for which they were not yet motivated to seek solutions. It is not until the mid-12th century that we have firm evidence for Watten Meer ship-types, in the shape of heavily constructed cogs, travelling along the west coast of Jutland.[29] The Scandinavian ship-types of the earlier centuries, especially the lightly built and heavily manned rowing vessels, might have been better suited for this type of coast than heavier ships were, as these could be beached and hauled ashore by their crews, and were not as dependent on the presence of sheltered anchorage in river mouths or behind protecting islands.

Based on the discussion above, John Haywood's theory regarding widespread naval and piratical activities by Franks, Frisians and Saxons, and some use of the sail by these groups, does not necessarily lead to the acceptance of an early adaptation of sail in Scandinavian ships as well. On the contrary, there seems to be good reason to maintain a late date for the introduction of this technology in Scandinavia. However, Haywood raises an important point: the Scandinavian raiders did not go to coasts where the inhabitants were unfamiliar with seafaring, or possessed inferior vessels, and their success is due to the failure of their counterparts to establish or maintain an efficient defence.[30] Moreover, this last point reveals the importance of knowing the character and capacity of Scandinavian ships in the early Viking Age, as it may also be our best source for understanding seafaring in other parts of Northern Europe.

Viking Age ships and seafaring in the West

Early Scandinavian sailing ships

As mentioned earlier, the Norwegian ship-graves dominate the group of early Viking Age ship-finds in Scandinavia that can be reconstructed with some accuracy. It is therefore of obvious interest to investigate how well the Tune, Gokstad and Oseberg ships represent the vessels that were actually used on voyages between Scandinavia and the west.

Frequently, since the excavation of the ships in the late 19th and early 20th centuries, various arguments have been used to claim that the grave finds should not be regarded as representative finds. Such a critique concentrates especially on the beautifully ornamented and not very sea-worthy Oseberg ship. Already in the 1917 publication, one of the excavators suggested that this ship had once been a pleasure vessel for inshore use, rather than a seagoing ship; he also argued that both the Oseberg and the Tune ship were old vessels, long since taken out of practical use when they were buried.[31] Others suggest that the Oseberg ship may have been exclusively a ceremonial vessel.[32] The thesis about the two ships being derelicts by the time of burial can now be rejected on the basis of dendrochronological investigations. The Oseberg, the Tune and the Gokstad ships have all been subject to careful examinations in order to date their time of both construction and deposition. The dendrochronological analyses show that both the Oseberg and the Gokstad ships had been in use for 10–15 years before they were buried in their secondary function as grave ships.[33] The Oseberg ship was constructed in *c.* AD 820, while the ship burial took place in AD 834. As for the Gokstad ship, a construction date of AD 895–900 was obtained, while the grave chamber was built around AD 905–910. The Tune ship was built *c.* AD 910, and its burial may have taken place between AD 910–920, when the ship was still almost new. Other finds of medieval, clinkerbuilt vessels demonstrate that such ships were in use for much longer periods and thus the three ships from Norway were by no means worn-out hulks by the time of deposition.

The two other points of critique are more difficult to counter. Experimental archaeology has demonstrated the seaworthiness of the Gokstad ship beyond doubt, as accurate copies of the vessel have crossed the Atlantic on several occasions.[34] The Norwegian Viking-ship expert Arne Emil Christensen has positively evaluated the seaworthiness of a full-scale copy of the Oseberg ship, while others are very critical.[35] Whatever the actual seaworthiness of the Oseberg ship, however, such discussions will always include a large degree of uncertainty, owing to the fact that we cannot judge today what risks seafarers were prepared to take in the Early Middle Ages. There can hardly be any doubt that under favourable conditions, the Oseberg ship would not have had any difficulties in covering the distance between southern Scandinavia and England – either along the coast or across the North Sea. The same thing can be said about the Tune ship, which, although contemporary with the Gokstad ship, is a much smaller and lighter vessel.

The excavators' interpretation of the Oseberg ship as a pleasure vessel is not based solely on their estimate of its seaworthiness. They had also observed that the planking of the deck had been treenailed to the beams over almost the entire ship. Only in the fore and aft, and at the mast, could the planks be removed in order to allow for bailing and access to the ballast. In the excavators' view this indicates that the possible cargo capacity of the ship was never exploited, making it unlikely that longer voyages were undertaken with the vessel. The argumentation is logical, although we may still ask what was gained from securing the deck in this manner? Not only the utilisation of the hold, but also the maintenance of the ship, including the inspection of sewn fastenings between the floor-timbers and the planking, was obstructed by the permanent deck.

Furthermore, it would be more difficult to empty the ship and thus reduce its weight before pulling it ashore. What motivated this solution? It is difficult to see that it would increase the level of comfort on board and thus facilitate the use of the vessel for pleasure or representative purposes. We could turn the argument upside down and speculate that the aim was to make access to the hold difficult, for some unknown reason – perhaps in order to limit the access to goods transported there. Another possible explanation is that fighting was considered such an important element of the ship's use that a stable deck was given priority over everyday use. Finally, securing the deck – which, after all, may not be original to the ship – can also be explained in a variety of ways not directly related to the sailing of the ship.

It has also been suggested that grave ships were built for ceremonial use. This is especially the case for the Oseberg ship, where the entire grave has been interpreted as the burial for a queen who had played a leading role in the fertility cult. According to this interpretation, put forward by Anne Stine Ingstad in 1994, the ship "is no ocean-going craft. The luxurious or-

Viking Age ships and seafaring in the West

namentation suggests that it may have been used for cultic service".[36] The grave inventory did indeed include several objects exclusively for ceremonial use, while the presence of other, everyday items is explained by Ingstad by their being bi-functional – of both practical and religious importance. Of importance for the interpretation of the ship is the beautifully decorated but functionally useless wagon.[37] It appears similar to those depicted in processions on a tapestry fragment in the grave, and some of its carvings can be related to the fertility cult.[38] The supposed poor sailing qualities of the vessel, combined with the fact that both the apparently ceremonial wagon and the ship are richly ornamented, thus lead Ingstad to the conclusion that the ship was ceremonial as well. Referring to the discussion above about seaworthiness, we may then want to discuss whether the carvings are enough to document the cultic character of the vessel? Ingstad does not analyse the carved motives on the ship, but they do not seem to contain any obvious references to the fertility myth, as was the case with the wagon. That carvings in their own right should imply a religious function appears unlikely, unless, perhaps, the amount of decoration is highly disproportionate to the object on which they are present – as in the case of the wagon, or the sledges that are also present in the find. We may ask, however, if the ornamentation found on the Oseberg ship is not exactly, what we should expect from a vessel belonging to the highest-ranking people in society in the 9th century? Taking into consideration the very significant amount of wealth invested in the construction of such a vessel, and the status that the ship gave its owner, there is no reason to be surprised by the presence of woodcarvings on the most prominent timbers of the vessel, fig. 5. Impressive as they are, the carvings restrict themselves to the stem and stern area, and only to such timbers that make up or are directly connected to the stem- and sternposts.[39] That the carvings on the ship only represent a small fragment of the vessel's total cost can be demonstrated by a small comparison based on experimental archaeology.

Fig. 5. The Oseberg ship as displayed in Oslo. The carvings on the stem are clearly visible. Both stems are decorated in the same manner. The uppermost part of the stem is also decorated on the side facing the interior of the ship, but there are no carvings outside the stem and stern area. After A.E. Christensen et al. (eds) 1992: 139.

Jan Bill

For the building of the Oseberg replica, two professional wood carvers were employed. Their entire work period, including frequent study trips to Oslo to study the original carvings, took six months each. Owing to the character of the trade, wood carvers basically use the same tools today as in the Viking Age, and power tools were only used sparingly in the process. It is therefore likely that the original carvings may also have taken altogether about twelve working months to produce.[40]

Such a process can be compared with the estimated time consumption for the production of a sail for a vessel of this size. In the Viking Age, the most commonplace material for sails is thought to have been wool. According to evidence from *c.* 1770, it took about 30 weeks of work to produce a woolen sail of *c.* 16 square metres with looms identical to those used in the Viking Age.[41] The Oseberg ship is believed to have had a sail of 86–110 m², which means that the production of the sail for the vessel alone represents about 3.5 years of work.[42] In terms of labour involved, the production of a sail was a significant investment, but even so it was only one component in the construction of a ship. Also more than half a kilometre of planks, hundreds of metres of timbers, mast and spars had to be made and transported to the building site; iron had to be extracted for the thousands of iron rivets and nails that were to be forged alongside with appropriate fittings and anchors, and oars and other pieces of equipment had to be carved. Hundreds of metres of rope for rigging were produced from bast collected in the woods, tar was made, and the ship itself had to be put together. Even without quantifying all this work, it is obvious that the carvings, in all their splendour, represent only a small percentage of the total labour investment in the ship. Apart from this, it should be noted that carvings are not unknown from other Scandinavian ship- and boat-finds, although those of the Oseberg ship are outstanding for their quality and extent. Already the Nydam boats show such decorative elements, as does the larger Kvalsund boat.[43] Indeed, decorative mouldings along plank and timber edges constitute a characteristic element in Scandinavian boat- and shipbuilding well into the 13th century.[44] Remains of painted or incised patterns for painting are also sometimes found on early Scandinavian ships, for example the Gokstad and the Ladby ships,[45] revealing another way in which vessels were decorated. Iconographic evidence from the early Viking Age, especially the Gotland picture stones, but also some of the Hedeby coins and also less official iconography, fig. 6, shows that the spiral-shaped stem and stern termi-

Jan Bill

Fig. 6. A whetstone fragment found in a 9th-century sunken hut in Löddeköpinge, Western Sweden. Length 105 mm. The depiction shows the characteristic Oseberg type of sternpost termination. Photo: Lunds Universitets Historiska Museet.

nations of the Oseberg ship represented a widespread phenomenon; can we be sure that this was not also the case with wood carvings, although these would only survive under very extraordinary preservation conditions?

It thus seems that neither the "pleasure vessel theory" nor the "ceremonial vessel theory" can be used to dismiss the Oseberg ship as a valid example of early 9th-century shipbuilding. It is even possible to argue, as has been done elsewhere, that as a sailing vessel the ship was unusually large for its time.[46] In short, this argumentation is based on the fact that in the Oseberg ship the keelson only spans two floor timbers, while in all later Viking ship-finds it spans three or more, with four as the minimum for vessels the size of Oseberg or larger, fig. 7. The distance between the floor timbers is dictated by the distance between the rowlocks, and is approximately one metre in all Scandinavian ships until well after the introduction of exclusively sail-driven vessels. This means that in smaller vessels, the solution chosen in the Oseberg ship may have functioned well, as the distance between two frames, and thus the length of the keelson, made up a larger proportion of the total length of the vessel; but as ship sizes grew, this proportion became smaller and smaller, until finally – between the construction of the Oseberg and the Gokstad ship – it was necessary to change the design principle, fig. 8.

	Dating (AD)	Length (metres)	Length of keelson (metres)	Number of frames under keelson	Keelson length in percentage of ship length	Reference
Finds in W. Scandinavia						
Oseberg	820	21.5	1.8	2	8	A.W. Brøgger, H. Falk, and H. Shetelig, 1917
Gokstad	895-900	23.2	3.7	4	16	A.W. Brøgger and H. Shetelig, 1951
Tune	c. 910	20	3.14	4	16	H. Shetelig, 1917: 13
Hedeby 2	c. 970-980	9-12	2.6	4	22-29	O. Crumlin-Pedersen, 1997a: 97
Hedeby 1	c. 985	30.9	3.4-4.5	5-6	11-15	O. Crumlin-Pedersen, 1997a: 90
Äskekärr 1	c. 1000	15.8	2.7	3	17	A. Bråthen, 1998: 14; P. Humbla, 1934
Hedeby 3	1025	c. 22	>5.40	>7	>25	O. Crumlin-Pedersen, 1997a: 100-102
Hasnæs 2	1040 (K-1097)	?	>2.5	>3	?	O. Crumlin-Pedersen, 1972: 70-71
Skuldelev 1	1030-1050	16.3	c. 4.0-5.1	5-6	25-31	O. Olsen and O. Crumlin-Pedersen, 1968: 106-107
Skuldelev 2	1042-1043	c. 30	13.3	19	44	O. Olsen and O. Crumlin-Pedersen, 1968: 115
Skuldelev 3	1030-1050	14	3.2	3	23	O. Olsen and O. Crumlin-Pedersen, 1968: 127
Skuldelev 5	1030-1050	17.5	3.7	5	21	O. Olsen and O. Crumlin-Pedersen, 1968: 141-142
Skuldelev 6	1030-1050	12	1.32	1	11	O. Olsen and O. Crumlin-Pedersen, 1968: 151
Roskilde 6	after 1025	c. 36	>5	>6	>14	J. Bill, M. Gøthche, and H.M. Myrhøj, 2000: 218-219

Fig. 7. Table showing the length of keelsons from AD 800-1100 in relation to ship lengths. All finds are dated by dendrochronology or 14C (cal.).

Fig. 8. Arrangements around the mast-step in the Oseberg (above) and Gokstad (below) ships. Drawing by Werner Karrasch, The Viking Ship Museum, Roskilde.

Jan Bill

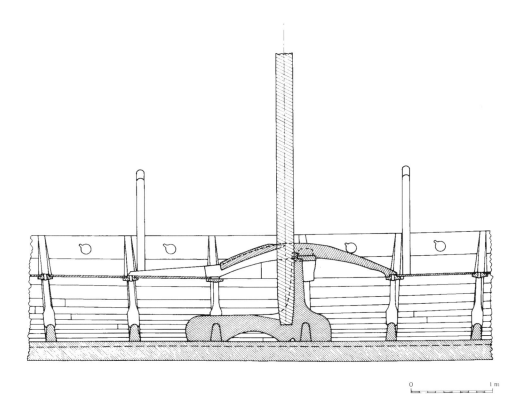

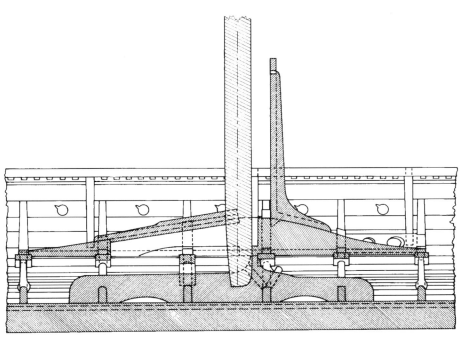

Viking Age ships and seafaring in the West

Discussion

Archaeology has brought to light a limited number of ship-finds that, through their reconstruction, have shed some light on the character of Scandinavian seafaring during the 8th–11th centuries. Combined with iconographic material, partly from the same period and partly from preceding centuries, it appears that shipbuilding developed very quickly in the Viking Age once sails became commonly used in larger ships from the 7th century. From the 8th–early 10th centuries, ships were combined rowing and sailing vessels and had a very limited cargo capacity. The Oseberg and Gokstad finds indicate that the size of sailing ships was increasing in the period. During the 9th century, large Scandinavian sailing ships were capable of transporting 40–60 men, while from the late 10th and the first half of the 11th century, figures from 60–100 men can be attested. These last figures agree with historical evidence from the first half of the 11th century that indicates that ships of Harold and Cnut in AD 1016, and those of Hardaknut a quarter of a century later, were manned by about 80 men.[47] Cargo capacity developed even more dramatically, but only after the introduction of specialised cargo carriers in the 10th century. By the first quarter of the 11th century, such ships could transport cargoes large enough to participate in bulk trade, although their construction may have served other purposes, such as providing safe vessels for North Atlantic voyages.

Both developments – that of enlarged capacity for transport of men and cargo – are important for discussing the Viking expansion into the west. However, the increase in seaworthiness of these vessels is of significance. For Scandinavians in the 8th and 9th centuries, expeditions to the west must have been fairly daring experiences: relatively small open vessels, in the beginning probably with a quite limited ability to survive severe weather, carried fairly small groups of men with few provisions. For the armies of the 10th and 11th centuries, the situation was somewhat different: larger, more seaworthy ships were available, carrying larger groups of men, and the possibility of including supply vessels in the fleet was now present. It may be assumed that the possibility of keeping a fleet of sailing ships together increases proportionally with the seaworthiness of the ships, as the risk of a ship being forced to break away and run before the wind to survive bad weather would decrease. It is impossible to quantify the effect of improvements in seaworthiness, but taken together with the increase in size, it ap-

Jan Bill

pears likely that the differences between early and late Viking expeditions in terms of size were substantial.

However, even a small fleet of perhaps five ships of Oseberg size could carry 200 men. According to minimalist military historians like Reuter, this was perhaps not a small army by early 9th-century standards.[48] Maybe the rapid development of Scandinavian shipbuilding during the Viking Age that is attested in the archaeological material reflects not only a general increase in Northern European trade, as is generally accepted today, but just as much an increase in the scale and complexity of military operations.

Notes

1 This article is also published in French in Flambard Héricher 2001.
2 See Crumlin-Pedersen & Munch Thye et al. 1995 for a collection of articles of the symbolic use of ships in Scandinavia from the Mesolithic to medieval times.
3 See e.g. Milne & Goodburn 1990: 632–634; McGrail 1993; Vlek 1987.
4 Early versions of this discussion can be found in my articles in Bill 1997: 182–201 and Bill et al. 1997: 49–81.
5 Reuter 1997: 35–36.
6 Shetelig 1917; Brøgger & Shetelig 1951: 147–150; Knut Paasche, Oslo, is presently preparing a new reconstruction of the Tune ship.
7 For a more thorough discussion of the formation process for the ship-archaeological record, see Crumlin-Pedersen 1985.
8 Alopaeus 1995.
9 On the Graveney Boat, see Fenwick 1978; on Utrecht, see Vlek 1987 and van de Moortel 2000.
10 McGrail 1993: 98–99.
11 Crumlin-Pedersen 1999: 16.
12 Crumlin-Pedersen 1999: 16–18. The preliminary reconstructions of the new 11th-century ship finds from Roskilde, wreck 3 and 6, do not noticeably change the picture of beam/length ratios, but it is worth mentioning that the Tune ship, contemporary with the Gokstad ship, has a ratio of 0.218, some 12% less than that of the Gokstad ship and 15% less than the Oseberg ship's. See Bill et al. 1998 and Shetelig 1917: 15.
13 For Klåstad, see Christensen & Leiro 1976 and Eriksen 1993; for Äskekärr, dendrochronological dates vary between the early 10th century and *c.* 1025 for the construction of the ship, depending on whether the keelson, which has provided the late date, is accepted as part of the original construction or not. See Bråthen 1998.
14 Fenwick 1978; Bill 1994: 58–59; Goodburn 1994: 101–103.
15 Milne & Goodburn 1990: 633–634.
16 Carver 1990; Hines 1984.
17 Haywood 1991.
18 Rodger 1998: 5, note 10.
19 Haywood 1991: 21, 65, 136.
20 Rieck & Crumlin-Pedersen 1988: 129–133.
21 Crumlin-Pedersen 1990: 111.
22 Brøgger, Falk & Shetelig 1917.
23 Varenius 1992: 80 ff.
24 Shetelig & Johannessen 1929.
25 Opedal 1998: 64–65; Christensen 1998.
26 Haywood 1991: 71.
27 Haywood 1991: 62, note 85 is by Haywood quoted as: "Nec quisquam adventum eorum [i.e. the Maratocupreni] cavere poterat inopinum, non destinata, sed varia petentium et longinqua, et quoquo ventus duxerat erumpentum: quam ob causam prae ceteris hostibus Saxones timentur ut repentini" (Ammianus Marcellinus, XXVIII. 2.12).
28 See for example various articles in Crumlin-Pedersen & Munch Thye (eds) 1995.
29 On the basis of dendrochronological analyses the Kollerup cog from *c.* 1150 and the Skagen cog, from *c.* 1200, appear to be built from timbers felled in the southernmost part of Denmark. Both finds were wrecked on the west coast of Jutland. See Daly et al. 2000 and Lønstrup & Nielsen 1995: 13.
30 Haywood 1991: 76, 134–135, 138.
31 Brøgger, Falk & Shetelig 1917: 341.
32 Ingstad 1995: 144; Crumlin-Pedersen 1997b: 189.
33 Bonde 1994.
34 Christensen 1996: 84.
35 Christensen 1996: 83, Angela M.A. Schuster 1991.
36 Ingstad 1995: 144.
37 On the functionality of the wagon, see Schovsbo 1987: 33–34.
38 Ingstad 1995: 144.
39 Brøgger, Falk & Shetelig 1917: 328.
40 I want to thank woodcarver Tore Nord, Nordfjordeid, for this information.
41 Andersen et al. 1989: 21.
42 B. Andersen & E. Andersen 1989: 244.
43 Nydam: Engelhardt 1865; see Rieck 2000 for later finds. Kvalsund: Shetelig & Johannessen 1929.
44 Varenius 1992: 183.
45 Christensen 1979; Thorvildsen 1957: pl. II.
46 Bill 1997: 187.
47 See Abels 1997: note 51.
48 Reuter 1997: 35–36.

References

Abels, R., "English Logistics and Military Administration, 871–1066: The Impact of the Viking Wars". In: A.N. Jørgensen & B. Clausen (eds), *Military Aspects of Scandinavian Society in a European Perspective, AD 1-1300. Papers from an International Research Seminar at the Danish National Museum, Copenhagen, 2-4 May 1996.* Publications from The National Museum Studies in Archaeology & History 2 (Copenhagen 1997), pp. 257–265.

Alopaeus, H., "Aspects of the Lapuri Find". In: O. Olsen et al. (eds), *Shipshape. Essays for Ole Crumlin-Pedersen on the occasion of his 60th anniversary February 24th 1995* (Roskilde 1995).

Andersen, B. & E. Andersen, *Råsejlet – Dragens Vinge* (Roskilde 1989).

Andersen, E. et al., *Uldsejl i 1000 år* (Roskilde 1989).

Bill, J., "Iron Nails in Iron Age and Medieval Shipbuilding". In: C. Westerdahl (ed.), *Crossroads in Ancient Shipbuilding. Proceedings of the Sixth International Symposium on Boat and Ship Archaeology. Roskilde 1991.* Oxbow Monograph 40 (Oxford 1994), pp. 55–64.

— "Ships and Seamanship". In: P. Sawyer (ed.), *Oxford Illustrated History of the Vikings* (Oxford 1997), pp. 182–201.

Bill, J. et al., *Dansk søfarts historie 1: Indtil 1588. Fra stammebåd til skib* (Copenhagen 1997).

Bill, J. et al., "Nordeuropas største skibsfund. Skibskirkegård under museumsøen i Roskilde". *Nationalmuseets Arbejdsmark* (Copenhagen 1998), pp. 136–158.

Bonde, N., "De norske vikingeskibsgraves alder. Et vellykket norsk-dansk forskningsprojekt". *Nationalmuseets Arbejdsmark* (Copenhagen 1994), pp. 128–147.

— "Roskildeskibene". In: T. Christensen & M. Andersen (eds), *Civitas Roscald – fra byens begyndelse* (Roskilde 2000).

Brøgger, A.W. et al., *Osebergfunnet*, vol. 1 (Kristiania 1917).

Brøgger, A.W. & H. Shetelig, *The Viking Ships. Their Ancestry and Evolution* (Oslo 1951).

Bråthen, A., "Datering av skeppet Äskekärr 1". *GASTen* 22 (1998), pp. 13–15.

Carver, M.O.H., "Pre-Viking Traffic in the North Sea". In: S. McGrail (ed.), *Maritime Celts, Frisians and Saxons. Papers presented to a conference at Oxford in November 1988.* CBA Research Report 71 (London 1990), pp. 117–125.

Christensen, A. E., "Gokstadskipets dekorative utstyr". *Universitetets Oldsaksamling, Jubileumsårbok 1979.* Universitetets Oldsaksamling, årbok (Oslo 1979), pp. 145–149.

— "Proto-Viking, Viking and Norse Craft. In: A.E. Christensen (ed.), *The Earliest Ships.* Conway's History of the Ship (London 1996), pp. 72–88.

— "Skipsrestene fra Storhaug og Grønhaug". In: A. Opedal (ed.), *De glemte skipsgravene. Makt og myter på Avaldsnes.* Ams-Småtrykk 47 (Stavanger 1998), pp. 206–220.

Christensen, A. E. & G. Leiro, "Klåstadskipet". *Vestfoldminne* (1976), pp. 2–17.

Crumlin-Pedersen, O., "Kællingen og kløften. Nogle jyske fund af kølsvin og mastefisk fra 800-1200 e.Kr". *Handels- og Søfartsmuseet på Kronborg. Årbog* (1972), pp. 63–80.

— "Ship Finds and Ship Blockages AD 800-1200". In: K. Kristiansen (ed.), *Archaeological formation processes. The representativity of archaeological remains from Danish Prehistory* (Copenhagen 1985), pp. 215–228.

— "The boats and ships of the Angles and Jutes. In: S. McGrail (ed.), *Maritime Celts, Frisians and Saxons. Papers presented to a conference at Oxford in November 1988.* CBA Research Report 71 (London 1990), pp. 98–116.

— 1997a. *Viking-Age Ships and Shipbuilding in Hedeby/Haithabu and Schleswig.* Ships and Boats of the North 2 (Schleswig and Roskilde 1997).

— 1997b. "Large and Small Warships of the North". In: A.N. Jørgensen & B. Clausen (eds), *Military Aspects of Scandinavian Society in a European Perspective, AD 1-1300. Papers from an International Research Seminar at the Danish National Museum, Copenhagen, 2-4 May 1996.* Publications from The National Museum Studies in Archaeology & History 2 (Copenhagen 1997), pp. 184–194.

— "Ships as indicators of trade in Northern Europe 600-1200". In: J. Bill & B. Clausen (eds), *Maritime Topography and the Medieval Town.* Publications from The National Museum Studies in Archaeology & History 4 (Copenhagen 1999), pp. 9–18.

Crumlin-Pedersen O. & Munch Thye (eds), *The Ship as Symbol in Prehistoric and Medieval Scandinavia. Papers from an International Research Seminar at the Danish National Museum, Copenhagen, 5th–7th May 1994.* Publications from The National Museum, Studies in Archaeology & History 1 (Copenhagen 1995).

Daly, A. et al., "New dendro dates for Danish medieval ships from Eltang and Kollerup". *Maritime Archaeology Newsletter from Roskilde, Denmark* 14 (2000).

Engelhardt, C., *Nydam Mosefund. 1859-1863* (Copenhagen 1865).

Eriksen, O. Hylleberg, "Dendrokronologisk undersøgelse af skibsvrag fra Klåstad, Norge". *Nationalmuseets Naturvidenskabelige Undersøgelser* 21 (Copenhagen 1993).

Fenwick, V., *The Graveney Boat: a Tenth-Century Find from Kent. Excavation and recording; interpretation of the boat remains and the environment; reconstruction and other research; conservation and display.* BAR International Series 53 (Oxford 1978).

Flambard Héricher, A.-M. (ed.), *Vikings, des raids à colonisation* (Rouen 2001).

Goodburn, D., "Anglo-Saxon Boat Finds from London, Are they English?" In: C. Westerdahl (ed.), *Crossroads in Ancient Shipbuilding. Proceedings of the Sixth International Symposium on Boat and Ship Archaeology, Roskilde 1991.* Oxbow Monograph 40 (Oxford 1994), pp. 97–104.

Haywood, J., *Dark Age Naval Power. A Reassessment of Frankish and Anglo-Saxon Seafaring Activity* (London 1991).

Hines, J., *The Scandinavian Character of Anglian England in the Pre-Viking Period.* British Archaeological Reports 8 (Oxford 1984).

Humbla, P., "Båtfyndet vid Äskekärr". *Göteborg och Bohuslän Fornminnesförenings Tidsskrift* (1934), pp. 1–21.

Ingstad, A.S., "The Interpretation of the Oseberg-find". In: O. Crumlin-Pedersen & Munch Thye (eds), *The Ship as Symbol in Prehistoric and Medieval Scandinavia. Papers from an International Research Seminar at the Danish National Museum, Copenhagen, 5th-7th May 1994.* Publications from The National Museum, Studies in Archaeology & History 1 (Copenhagen 1995), pp. 139–147.

Lønstrup, J. & I. Nielsen, *Skagen. Den tilsandede Kirke* (Skagen 1995).

McGrail, S., *Medieval Boat and Ship Timbers from Dublin.* Medieval Dublin Excavations 1962–81. Ser. B., Vol. 3 (Dublin 1993).

Moortel, A. van de, "The Utrecht ship – was the log boat base expanded?" *Maritime Archaeology Newsletter from Roskilde, Denmark* 14 (2000), pp. 36–39.

Montelius, O., "Der Handel in der Vorzeit". *Prähistorische Zeitschrift* 2 (Berlin 1910), pp. 249–291.

Milne, G. and D. Goodburn, "The early medieval port of London AD 700-1200". *Antiquity* 64 (1990), pp. 629–636.

Olsen, O. & O. Crumlin-Pedersen, "The Skuldelev Ships. A report of the final underwater excavation in 1959 and the salvaging operation in 1962". *Acta Archaeologica* 38 (Copenhagen 1968), pp. 73–174.

Opedal, A., *De glemte skipsgravene. Makt og myter på Avaldsnes.* Ams-Småtrykk 47 (Stavanger 1998).

Reuter, T., "The recruitment of armies in the Early Middle Ages: what can we know?" In: A.N. Jørgensen & B. Clausen (eds), *Military Aspects of Scandinavian Society in a European Perspective, AD 1-1300. Papers from an International Research Seminar at the Danish National Museum, Copenhagen, 2-4 May 1996.* Publications from The National Museum Studies in Archaeology & History 2 (Copenhagen 1997), pp. 32–37.

Rieck, F., "Die Schiffahrt im Nordseegebiet, 250-850 n. Chr". In: Kramer et al. (eds), *Könige der Nordsee, 250-850 n. Chr.* (Leeuwarden 2000), pp. 55–66.

Rieck, F. & O. Crumlin-Pedersen, *Både fra Danmarks oldtid* (Roskilde 1998).

Rodger, N.A.M., *The Safeguard of the Sea. A Naval History of Britain 660-1649* (New York 1998).

Schovsbo, P.O., *Oldtidens vogne i Norden* (Frederikshavn 1987).

Schuster, A.M.A., "The Vikings Are Coming". *Archaeology* (1991), pp. 22–30.

Shetelig, H., *Tuneskibet.* Avhandlinger utgit av Universitetets Oldsaksamling II (Kristiania 1917).

Shetelig, H. & F. Johannessen, *Kvalsundfundet og andre norske Myrfund av Fartøier* (Bergen 1929).

Thorvildsen, K., *Ladbyskibet.* Nordiske Fortidsminder VI.1 (Copenhagen 1957).

Varenius, B., *Det nordiska skeppet. Teknologi och samhällsstrategi i vikingatid och medeltid.* Stockholm Studies in Archaeology 10 (Stockholm 1992).

Vlek, R., *The Mediaeval Utrecht Boat. The history and evaluation of one of the first nautical archaeological excavations and reconstructions in The Low Countries.* BAR International Series 382 (Oxford 1987).

Egge Knol

Frisia in Carolingian times

Introduction

There is quite a lot of written evidence of Viking presence in the northern Netherlands in Carolingian times. For example, it is known that in the middle of the 9th century the western part of the Netherlands was for some time given in fief to a Danish chieftain, Roric (Henderikx 1995; Besteman 1999, 2004). Several raids on the Frisian coasts during the 9th century are recorded. The trading settlement of Dorestad and other settlements along the Rhine formed important targets (van Es & Hessing 1994; Simek & Engel 2000). The Vikings were interested also in the rich coastal area along the Frisian coast. This is reason enough to discuss this particular coastline of the southern North Sea. The Dutch coast of the North Sea can be divided into three parts: the modern province of Zealand around the estuary of the Scheldt; the coast from the mouth of the river Meuse to the isle of Texel; and the northern Netherlands' salt-marsh area of the provinces Friesland and Groningen. This last-mentioned area is well known for the settlements built on artificial mounds, the so-called *wierden* or *terpen*, and has been the subject of recent studies.

The landscape in the northern Netherlands

The northern Netherlands consisted of the Wadden Sea – more or less the same as today – and a very extensive salt-marsh area. This area was not protected by dykes as it is today, but was open to the sea. During storms the area was flooded, and every time this happened sedimentation took place. It kept the soil fertile for salt-resistant vegetation. The area was split up by numerous estuaries, creeks and small rivers. These were the watercourses draining the land. Further inland was a vast peat area. The transition zone between the marsh and the peat lay relatively low and was flooded in wintertime. Here marine deposits partly covered the peat. To the south the peat bordered the Pleistocene hinterland. The hinterland was connected with the littoral by several sand ridges. The river Ems and some smaller riv-

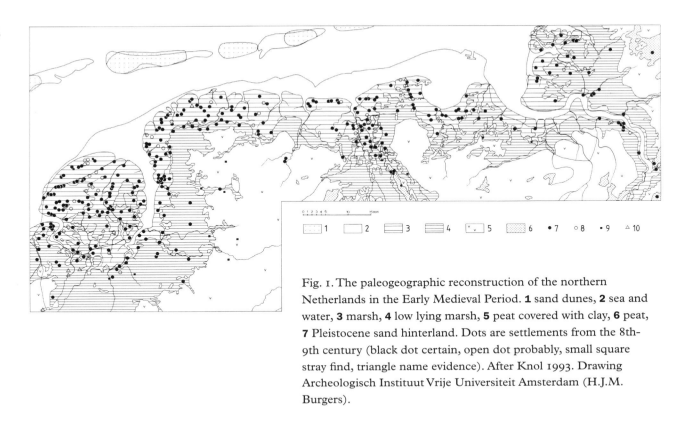

Fig. 1. The paleogeographic reconstruction of the northern Netherlands in the Early Medieval Period. **1** sand dunes, **2** sea and water, **3** marsh, **4** low lying marsh, **5** peat covered with clay, **6** peat, **7** Pleistocene sand hinterland. Dots are settlements from the 8th-9th century (black dot certain, open dot probably, small square stray find, triangle name evidence). After Knol 1993. Drawing Archeologisch Instituut Vrije Universiteit Amsterdam (H.J.M. Burgers).

ers like the Hunze, Aa, Lauwers and Boorne provided drainage of the peat (Knol 1993), fig. 1.

In response to increasingly frequent flooding, the local population from around the year 500 BC onwards built artificial mounds to live upon, known as *terpen*, *wierden* or (in Germany) *Wurten*. These *terpen* were not permanently populated. A lack of datable finds seems to suggest that the majority of the *terpen* were not inhabited in the 4th century AD (Taayke 1996). During the 5th century the population increased in the sparsely populated area. Most probably, this was partly through immigration of the so-called Anglo-Saxons, who on their way to England found an almost empty land attractive for settlement. The large salt-marsh area was the largest natural pasture in Europe. On the highest parts in this landscape, often near to the *terp*, small-scale arable farming was possible too. To protect the fields

Egge Knol

against the seawater, small low dykes were built (Bazelmans et al. 1999). The natural resources of this area, especially for cattle and sheep breeding, as well as the possibilities of transportation, were very good. They were the main reasons for living in a relatively inhospitable landscape.

In the 11th century the situation changed dramatically. New dykes protected the marsh from the sea. People were able to settle in the low parts of the marsh and some *terpen* were completely or partly abandoned. A second change was that the peat area south of the marsh became colonised. Continuous accumulation of organic material in the *terpen* had made the soil of these mounds very fertile. In the 19th century people started to quarry the soil, which was used as a fertiliser. It gave rise to a flourishing industry and, as a result, most of the terpen were dug away, partly or indeed completely. During these excavations archaeological finds were handed over to provincial museums and preliminary observations were published. Archaeological excavations in the 20th century have revealed a great deal of the history of habitation in the salt-marsh area from 600 BC until recent times. This paper deals solely with the evidence from Carolingian times.

The settlements along the coast

The early-medieval houses were often aisled farmhouses with walls of sods. *Grubenhäuser* were very common in the settlements of that time. No complete early-medieval settlement has been excavated in the marsh area, but available evidence suggests that there could have been several farms on a larger *terp*. At Leens, one farmhouse was rebuilt seven times on the same spot (Van Giffen 1940), fig. 3. Walls of the houses were made of sod; therefore, the site rapidly grew in height. This kind of building was also responsible for a marked enlargement of the *terpen*. The agricultural output was the main source of existence, but all kind of handicrafts, like pottery-making, weaving, smithing, goldsmithing, comb-making, tanning, glass-bead making and woodworking have been documented (e.g. Roes 1963; Tempel 1969; Bos et al. 1999). Leather, wool and bone were available locally. Wood, antler and natural stone, including flint, were imported from the Pleistocene hinterland. Amber was probably collected on the coastal islands (Waterbolk & Waterbolk 1991). Raw materials for producing items of bronze, iron, precious metals and glass were imported from other areas.

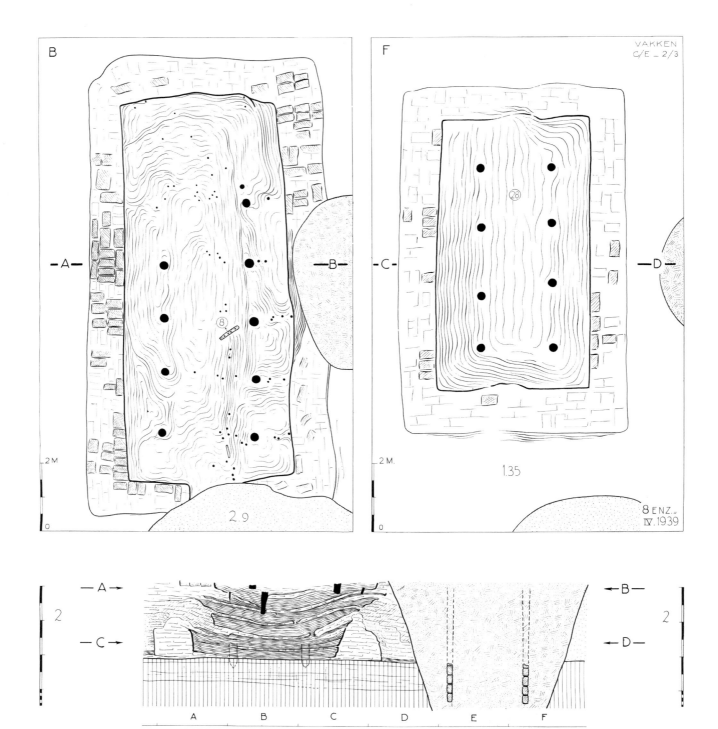

Contributors

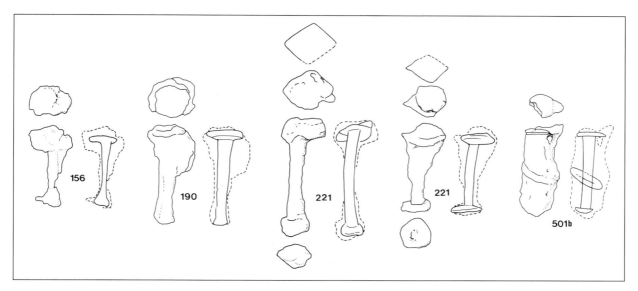

Fig. 2. Some iron clinkers found in the cemetery Oosterbeintum 6th–early 8th century. Figure after Knol et al. 1996. Drawing Archeologisch Instituut Vrije Universiteit Amsterdam (H.J.M. Burgers).

Exchange and importing goods from abroad

Commercial quarrying and archaeological research in the coastal areas have revealed a lot of imported goods. Wheel-thrown pottery and coins point to contacts with the Frankish realm along the Rhine. Disc-on-bow brooches, bracteates and other jewellery show connections with the English and the Scandinavian regions. Whalebone weaving battens may represent a connection with the Norwegian area. In a grave at Ferwerd a panther cowry was found. A stray find of this cowry species turned up in a *terp* at or near Lekkum and a tiger cowry at Adorp (Knol 2006). These cowries live only in the Red Sea and the Gulf of Aden and, therefore, had travelled a long way to the Frisian coast (Knol 1993). A specific group of finds are coins. Frankish as well as Byzantine coins suggest exchange. This exchange went

Fig. 3. Section of the terp Tuinster wierde Leens. The floors and sod-walls of seven farms can be seen. After Van Giffen 1940. Drawing University of Groningen, Groningen Institute of Archaeology.

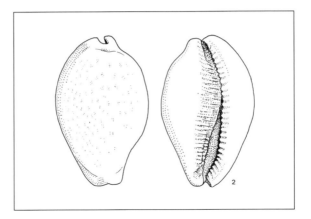

Fig. 4. Cowry shell found in grave Ferwerd Burmania I, 6th/7th century. After Knol 1993. Drawing Archeologisch Instituut Vrije Universiteit Amsterdam (H.J.M. Burgers).

partly through trade, but gift-exchange and looting should not be ruled out either. Products of animal husbandry were commodities for export.

During Carolingian times the Frisians were known as sailors plying around the western world, but so far the archaeological evidence of navigation along the northern coast is almost exclusively circumstantial. Recovered items, however, suggest that at least some international exchange must have taken place. Several dozen clinker nails found in the cemetery of Oosterbeintum and the settlement of Wijnaldum are the only surviving evidence of shipbuilding techniques (Knol et al. 1996), fig. 2, as wood was rare in the marsh, and most old wood, including parts of old ships, would have been used as fuel; as a result very little wood has survived.

Burial customs in the northern Netherlands

A lot of information is available about burial customs, thanks to excavations of cemeteries at Hogebeintum (Boeles 1951), Oosterbeintum (Knol et al. 1996), Ezinge-De Bouwerd (Knol 2007) and Godlinze (Van Giffen 1920), as well as to many stray finds and observations, fig. 4. The dead were either buried or cremated. Both rituals were practiced in the same period. After a cremation the remains of the pyre were collected in an urn and buried in the same cemetery as inhumations. Some of the dead were laid in coffins made of hollowed oak. Buried bodies lie with legs extended or flexed. Quite often the dead were provided with grave goods, laid in the urns or graves. Jewellery, weapons, pottery and amulets were among the grave goods. In several cemeteries graves of male dogs and horses are documented. However, neither the number nor the nature of the grave goods can be called rich in comparison with those of the funerary tradition in the central Netherlands. Cemeteries such as Wageningen (van Es 1964) and Lent (van Es & Hulst 1991) produced considerably more rich graves and finer grave goods. The size of the cemeteries indicates small communities of about 8 to 10 families.

Local differences in find patterns

The northern Dutch coastal zone can be divided into several areas that were not equal in wealth (wealth as seen in the archaeological record). The distribution of gold coins, jewellery and hoards that are dated to the 6th and 7th centuries leads to a hypothesis that the northern half of Westergo was the centre of Frisian power. The distribution of imported wheel-thrown pottery confirms this assumption. In Oostergo wheel-thrown pottery is not common and in Groningen it is scarce. But in Westergo this kind of pottery is very common. Owing to the poor archaeological record of the western coastal area, it is uncertain whether Westergo was really the richest part of the early-medieval Netherlands. Imported wheel-thrown pottery is very common in the western part of the Netherlands too. Indeed, the early-medieval sites of Texel and Wieringen were detected through this pottery (Woltering 2000; Knol 1993; Nicolay 2003). It is not impossible that our view regarding the distribution of objects made of precious metals is biased by metal-detector finds, because northern Westergo is more suitable for detector work owing to its arable farming (see Bazelmans et al. 1999). However, the distribution of wheel-thrown pottery is not biased by metal-detector finds. The quality of the objects and the amount of hoards in the northern Westergo region is so much higher than in the other areas that any bias due to detector finds cannot explain the differences.

The 8th century: A century of wars

In the 7th century, chieftains of the Frisian regions gained a lot of power in the central Netherlands, and even conquered Dorestad. After the death of the Frisian king Radbod in 719, the estuaries of the large rivers and today's West-Friesland were conquered by the Franks, followed by annexation of

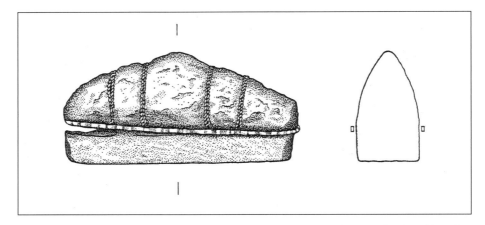

Fig. 6. Sword-pommel spatha type K, found in Maarhuizen. Private collection. Drawing University of Groningen, Groningen Institute of Archaeology (J.M. Smit).

Westergo and Oostergo after the Battle of the Boorne in 734. After the killing of Boniface (754) and the uprising under Widukind (780s), the eastern regions too came under Frankish control. It would be interesting to see if any traces of these conquests can be found in the archaeological record.

It is surprising that in spite of all the signs of a prosperous country, weapon graves were virtually unknown in Merovingian times. Yet in the 8th century and early 9th century there is a sudden boom in the northern Netherlands of graves containing double-edged swords (*spatha*), single-edged swords (*langsax*), stirrups, spearheads and/or drinking cups made of glass (Ypey 1982, 1984; Knol 1993), fig. 6. Presumably, the excavated graves of horses and dogs also belonged to such burials. Buried dogs were always large male specimens that may well have been war-dogs (Knol 1993; Knol et al. 1996; Prummel 1992). Many graves contained just a single item. Occasionally a grave contains two or more grave goods, e.g. a *langsax* and a cup at Ferwerd-Burmania, or a *spatha*, a spearhead and a folding knife at Hogebeintum (grave 42), fig. 7. In 1906 a single grave at Antum was said to have contained a *spatha*, stirrups, a short sword and three spearheads, but due to poor documentation of this find, this information is not altogether reliable (van Es 1971; Miedema 1983 esp. pp. 209–213). In Godlinze four cremation graves and one inhumation contained weapons. The inhumation contained just a *langsax*, but the cremation graves contained several pieces

Egge Knol

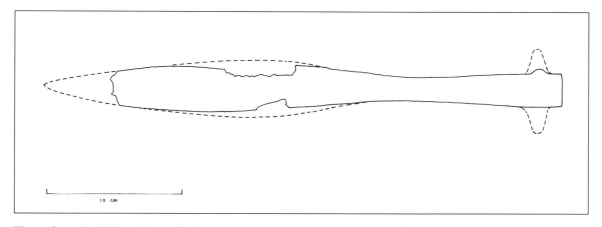

Fig. 7. Spearhead Maarhuizen. Collection Groninger Museum 1994-IV-1. Drawing University of Groningen, Groningen Institute of Archaeology (J.M. Smit).

of equipment including *spathas*, *umbos* and stirrups. Unfortunately, it is not possible to establish the exact content of these graves (Knol & Bardet 1999). In all, 31 inhumations and five cremation graves with 8th-century weapons, glass cups or horses have been found in the region of salt marshes and *terpen* in the northern Netherlands.

Similar graves with one or several Carolingian weapons have also been found outside the coastal region of the northern Netherlands: in the western, central and eastern Netherlands, as well as in adjoining northern Germany (Knol & Bardet 1999; Laux 1987; Westphal 2002). A check shows that weapons of the same type appear both with inhumations and with cremations. Furthermore, it is interesting to note that in the coastal regions of the northern Netherlands and northern Germany several graves with weapons may appear in a single cemetery. There are only very few if any clear chronological differences between these graves. At Schortens, a double weapon grave was found: a single grave containing two bodies, each with weapons (Herrmann & Rötting 1983). Evidently more than one individual at a time may have been eligible for burial with weapons. Occasionally, weapon graves lie isolated or in a small cluster, while elsewhere in the *terp* there is a separate early-medieval cemetery. Although these observations were made a while ago, there is no reason to doubt their accuracy (Knol 1993: 165, 168).

After this description of the nature of the weapon graves – so far as we know, all men's graves – it is clear that in the short period of less than a hundred years remarkably many grave goods point to a martial lifestyle (weapons) and a fondness of feasting (glass cups). Yet there is no reason to assume that before or after the 8th century the local elite favoured a different lifestyle. Evidently, conditions in the 8th century required one to emphasise one's status also by means of funerary practice. Burial or cremation was part of the ritual that assisted the dead to enter the realm of the ancestors. Living relatives believed that the ancestors were still able to intervene in their lives (Bazelmans 1999). Weapon burials referred to positions and values of the future rather than positions of the past. Weapon graves are strongly associated with episodes of intense rivalry in a rapidly changing society (Theuws 2009). So it is plausible to link the large number of weapon graves dated to the 8th century with the Frankish conquests.

Buried in weapon graves of this kind were, perhaps, both the opponents of the Franks and their local allies. By means of a conspicuously martial, non-Christian funeral the relatives could state their opposition to the Frankish conquerors. Cremating the dead had been banned by the Church and gradually became obsolete under Frankish rule (Knol 1993). This could be a definite incentive for opponents of the Franks to opt for cremation rather than inhumation. Maybe this is why no fewer than four weapon graves at Godlinze contained cremated remains.

But we might also imagine that the weapons accompanied village headmen appointed by the Frankish rulers. Their authority would not have extended beyond the village level, since there may be several weapon graves in one cemetery and none of these graves are particularly rich. It is possible that the relatives of the local headman used a conspicuous funeral with weapons to emphasise the powerful position of their family. They might have been followers of the Frankish kings who were rewarded with land or authority, but alternatively they might have been traditional local leaders who, by swearing allegiance to the new overlords, saw their land rights or authority affirmed. This could explain the occurrence of such graves in regions that had been conquered by the Franks at an earlier date, such as Zuid-Holland and the central Netherlands. It may be significant that on several occasions weapon graves were found within or near churchyards (Valkenburg, Marrum – *terp* Roorda, Maarhuizen). The Church did not approve of grave goods, but did not deal harshly with transgressors as it

Egge Knol

did in the case of cremation. It is possible that both explanations apply simultaneously, as reactions to each other. The relatives of the Franks' opponents may well have expressed their abhorrence of the Franks by upholding various pagan customs. The practice of burying weapons at their funerals would have emphasised the power of the survivors, the dead person and the ancestor that the dead person had now become; whereas new local leaders could have felt the need to underline their acquired or strengthened position also by burying weapons. After the whole area had been under Frankish rule for some time, the position of the new elite was no longer contested. Demonstrative mortuary ritual and burying weapons as a political statement were no longer necessary. This line of reasoning may explain both the lack of weapon graves before the Frankish conquests and the eventual disappearance of the practice.

The arrival of Christianity

The Franks had adopted Christianity, and in the wake of their armies, missionaries traversed the conquered territories to spread their faith. The change to Christianity is only vaguely detectable in the archaeological record. The oldest traces of churches go back to the 9th century. The tradition of cremating the dead was banned by the Church. In the east it persisted longer than in the west. This is in accordance with the historical fact that western Frisia was Christianised earlier. It is remarkable that in the 9th century brooches with Christian symbols like crosses and saints were very common in the northern Netherlands. Perhaps they were used as a visible sign of Christianity. Keys with crosses are known too. In the transitional process that Christianisation must have been, some retention of ancient practices is not unlikely.

The western coastal area

Having discussed the situation in the northern coastal area in this paper, I feel that some remarks on the western coastal area are necessary as well.

The coast consisted of a large area of marshland behind a broad zone of dunes (Woltering et al. 1999). These dunes were cut through by estuaries of the river Meuse, the river Rhine, and more to the north some small rivers. Along the mouths of these rivers, fluvial deposits as well as marine deposits were creating fertile land. More to the north in this Holocene landscape were the Pleistocene outcrops of the future islands of Texel and Wieringen. Behind the coastal dunes was a very wide marshy area. Colonisation of this marshland started in Carolingian times on the levees along the small rivers. Later, oxidation of the peat forced people to move further inland. To the east of the large marsh was an inland sea, Almere (later known as Zuiderzee). It was part of the access route to Dorestad in the central Netherlands. Along this route lay the Carolingian port of Medemblik (Besteman 1990).

Large parts of the dunes were eroded in later times, while other parts of the dunes became covered in the course of subsequent medieval dune-formation. Unfortunately, the archaeological record is therefore fragmentary. But available records give a picture of the populated coastal area. The dunes and especially the estuaries were densely populated, as were the Pleistocene outcrops of Texel and Wieringen (Woltering 2000). There was a round stronghold on Texel from the 7th century onward. Although this conjecture is not directly supported by further finds, Texel must have been an important centre of power (Woltering 2002). Through time, a progressively larger part of the marshland was populated. The finds in this part of the Netherlands were the subject of a study by the "Frisia" project (Heidinga 1997; Bazelmans et al. 2002). It is clear that habitation in this region was more important than has been assumed until recently. The area around the rivers Meuse and Rhine were probably the core territory of the famous Frisian kings Aldgisl and Radbod. After all, by controlling these estuaries it was possible to control the mainstream of transport into Europe. It was in this region that the Danish chieftain Roric held sway in the middle of the 9th century. The two hoards of Carolingian coins and Viking jewellery found at Westerklif on the island of Wieringen are related to this period. These hoards included coins and hack silver and had a number of other characteristics typical of Viking hoards (Besteman 1999, 2002, 2004).

In the Early Middle Ages the estuary of the river Scheldt consisted of a marsh area behind a narrow strip of dunes. The marsh was split up by a range of gullies and streams, as well as by the Scheldt. The dunes were densely populated and in the dunes of the isle of Walcheren there was a trading centre *Walichrum*. This trading centre was raided by the Vikings. The marsh area behind the dunes was sparsely populated, but intensively used for sheep rearing. This particular area became inhabited in later times (Van Heeringen et al. 1995; Vos & Van Heeringen 1996).

The Viking threat

The Vikings directed their efforts primarily towards the Rhine and the trading settlements along this river, including Dorestad, the renowned early medieval emporium (van Es & Hessing 1994; Simek & Engel 2000; Verwers in this volume; Willemsen 2004). In the past few years, new evidence has become available on the Viking raids along the Rhine. It is clear that the invasion of 882 via the Rhine and the IJssel also reached the towns of Zutphen and Deventer. In response, both towns were fortified with ramparts (Bartels 2006; Fermin & Groothedde 2006). As another reaction to these raids, ring forts were constructed in the southwestern Netherlands (Van Heeringen et al. 1995).

Until recently, archaeological evidence of the presence of the Vikings, either as raiders or as temporary settlers in the northern Netherlands, went unrecognised. A few stray finds discovered along the west coast were the only exception, fig. 5. But recently the two abovementioned silver hoards on the isle of Wieringen were connected with the Vikings. These finds place all kind of separate finds – particularly countless detector finds – in a new perspective. Arabic coins, several metal objects with Scandinavian motifs, all fit into a period in which the western Netherlands were in fief to a Viking ruler (Besteman 2004). In the northeastern part of the Netherlands, there are few indications of Viking fiefdom. It is known that a Norseman who had converted to Christianity led a force against Roric in Oostergo in 873 (Blok 1978). From 826 until 852, another Norseman had land in fief in Riustingen, which lies more to the east, in adjoining Germany.

Metal detectors are increasingly bringing to light various metallic items, including Arabic coins. The most remarkable of these are the many hoards from the 9th century, which are currently being found in the northern coastal area. The large number of these 9th-century hoards gives rise to conjectures about a correlation with the raids of the Norsemen along the coasts of the North Sea. Boeles (1915) compiled an overview of the Carolingian treasures that were known to him. However, he was not always able to study the composition of these hoards.

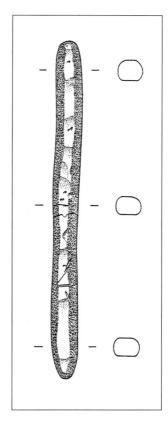

Fig. 5. Silver ingot stray find in a terp near Warffum. Collection Groninger Museum inv. no. 1999-III-5. Drawing University of Groningen, Groningen Institute of Archaeology (J.M. Smit).

There is a suspicion that there must have been many more. The hoards can vary from several dozen to hundreds of silver coins, occasionally supplemented with gold imitation *solidi* or jewellery. However, the emphasis lies on silver coinage. The largest hoard, discovered at Tzummarum in 1991, consists of approximately 2800 coins! From the Frisian and Groningen coastal region, thirteen hoards that were buried between 816 and 915 are currently known. Moving along the coast, these sites were at Pingjum – Kimswerd (2x), Achlum, Tzummarum, Winsum, Aalzum and Oudwoude in Friesland and Lutke Saaksum, Siuksum, Marsum, Woldendorp, Wagenborgen and an unknown site in the province of Groningen. Beyond the so-called *kweldergebied* (the saltmarsh area), but not too distant, hoards have also been found at Rijs in Gaasterland, Nuis in Westerkwartier, Midlaren and Zuidlaren in northern Drenthe, and at Holtland just across the German border (Kreis Leer) (Haertle 1997; Pol 1992). In view of the distribution of 9th-century silver hoards in Western Europe, this is a remarkable concentration. The distribution of these Carolingian treasures is fairly even across the northern coastal area, in contrast to the 7th century, the time when Westergo was notably wealthier than the littoral further east (Knol 1993; Nicolay 2003). The number of hidden hoards is substantially greater than in the previous centuries, while there is no reason to assume that the Carolingian hoards stood a greater chance of being recovered than other treasures.

There are two possible explanations for this concentration of hoards. Both may apply to the situation. Of course it is possible that a hoard was buried by an owner who saw no opportunity to recover it, perhaps because of being killed or captured by a Norseman. However, there may also be another explanation. The other explanation is that of the votive offering. Perhaps the hidden hoards of inland Rijs, Nuis, Midlaren, Zuidlaren and Holtgaste fall into this category. The explanation is also plausible for older treasures, from the Merovingian era for example. In general, votive sacrifices were placed in wet contexts (rivers and bogs). But in the coastal area, life was conducted entirely within the universe of the so-called *wierde* (artificial dwelling mound). A sacrificial spot near a house is therefore not so surprising.

It remains an open question as to who made such votive offerings. The Frankish kings had conquered the northern Netherlands in the course of the 8th century, and the missionaries followed in their wake. The superficial Christianisation of the northern Netherlands was completed in

Egge Knol

the 9th century, but pre-Christian beliefs would probably not have disappeared entirely by then. With the threat of the Norsemen, it is perfectly plausible that people should make sacrifices to the old, familiar gods. Eight of the silver hoards were hidden in the period between 850 and 875, i.e. in the time of Roric and his son Godfried.

It is a great pity that so few sources from the 9th century have survived, because the presence of the Norsemen may certainly have been much more substantial than currently imagined. Indeed, maybe the abovementioned whalebone weaving battens and the whalebone staff could be an indication of Vikings in the region. The staff, fig. 8, which is engraved with a runic inscription, dates from the 9th century and has remained without a parallel right until the present (Knol & Looijenga 1990).

Whatever may have been the influence of the Vikings on the northern Dutch coastal area, the archaeological evidence points to a prosperous country. I should like to close this paper by outlining an intriguing phenomenon. From the 8th and especially from the 9th century onwards and throughout the 10th century, large areas of peat were reclaimed. During the 9th and 10th centuries the peat areas were populated. It is tempting to speculate that it was the threat posed by the Vikings which made people move inland into this inhospitable area.

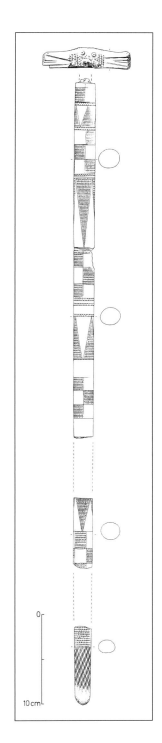

Fig. 8. T-Staff found in the terp of Bernsterburen. Made of a bone of a whale with an inscription in Anglo-Frisian runes, 8th century. Collection Fries Museum Leuwarden. Drawing University of Groningen, Groningen Institute of Archaeology (H.R. Roelink).

Frisia in Carolingian times

References

Bartels, M. *De Deventer wal tegen de Vikingen, archeologisch en historisch onderzoek naar de vroegmiddeleeuwse wal en stadsmuren (850–1900) en een vergelijking met andere vroegmiddeleeuwse omwalde nederzettingen*. Rapportages archeologie Deventer 18 (Deventer 2006).

Bazelmans, J., *By Weapons Made Worthy. Lords, Retainers and Their Relationship in Beowulf*. Amsterdam Archaeological Studies (Amsterdam 1999).

Bazelmans, J., D. Gerrets & A. Pol., "Metaaldetectie en het Friese Koninkrijk". *De Vrije Fries* 78 (1998), pp. 9–48.

Bazelmans, J., D. Gerrets, J. de Koning & P. Vos., "Zoden aan de dijk". *De Vrije Fries* 79 (1999), pp. 7–74.

Bazelmans, J., M. Dijkstra & J. de Koning, "Holland in het eerste millenium". In: T. de Nijs & E. Beukers (eds), *Geschiedenis van Holland* 1 (Hilversum 2002), pp. 21–68.

Besteman, J.C., "North Holland AD 400–1200: turning tide or tide turned?" In: J.C. Besteman, J.M. Bos & H.A. Heidinga (eds), *Medieval Archaeology in the Netherlands: Studies presented to H.H. van Regteren Alten*. SPP, 4 (Assen and Maastricht 1990), pp. 91–120.

— "Viking silver on Wieringen". In: H. Sarfatij et al. (eds), *In Discussion with the Past. Archaeological Studies Presented to W.A. van Es* (Zwolle 1999), pp. 253–266.

— "Viking Silver Hoard from Westerklief in the Former Isle of Wieringen (Province North Holland) in the Light of the Viking Relations with Frisia". In: H. Sarfatij, W.J.H. Verwers & P.J. Woltering (eds), *In Discussion with the Past. Archaeological Studies Presented to W.A. van Es* (Zwolle 1999), pp. 253–266.

— "Nieuwe Vikingvondsten van Wieringen: de zilverschat Westerklief II". In: P.J. Woltering, W.J.H. Verwers & G.J. Scheepstra (eds), *Middeleeuwse toestanden, archeologie, geschiedenis en monumentenzorg* (Hilversum 2002), pp. 65–75.

— "Scandinavisch gewichtsgeld in Nederland in de Vikingperiode". In: E.H.P. Cordfunke & H. Sarfatij (eds), *Van Solidus tot Euro, geld in Nederland in economisch-historisch en politiek perspectief* (Hilversum 2004), pp. 21–40.

Besteman, J.C., J.M. Bos, D.A. Gerrets, H.A. Heidinga & J. de Koning, *The Excavations at Wijnaldum 1* (Rotterdam and Brookfield 1999).

Blok, D.P., "De wikingen in Friesland". *Naamkunde* 10 (1978), pp. 25–47.

Boeles, P.C.J.A., "Les trouvailles de nommaies carolingiennes dans les Pays-Bas, spécialement celles des trois provinces septentrionales". *Jaarboek van het Koninklijk Nederlandsch Genootschap voor Munt- en Penningkunde* 2 (1915), pp. 1–98.

— *Friesland tot de elfde eeuw, zijn vóór- en vroege geschiedenis* (The Hague 1951).

Es, W.A. van., "Het rijengrafveld van Wageningen". *Palaeohistoria* 10 (1964), pp. 181–316 & pl. XLVIII–LIV.

— "Antum". In: *Reallexicon der germanische Altertümer* 1 (3) (Berlin and New York 1971), pp. 361–362.

Es, W.A. van & R.S. Hulst, *Das merowingische Gräberfeld von Lent*. Nederlandse oudheden 14 (Amersfoort 1991).

Es, W.A. van & W.A.M. Hessing. *Romeinen Friezen en Franken in het hart van Nederland* (Utrecht 1994).

Fermin, B. & M. Groothedde, *De Zutphense ringwalburg van de 9e tot de 14e eeuw. Nieuwe gegevens en inzichten uit archeologisch onderzoek en boringen op de Zutphense markten*. Zutphense Archeologische Publicaties 22 (Zutphen 2006).

Giffen, A.E. van, "Een Karolingisch grafveld bij Godlinze". In: *Jaarverslag van de Verening voor Terpenonderzoek* 3–4 (1920), pp. 39–96 & pl. 0–XVI.

— "Een systematisch onderzoek in een der Tuinster wierden te Leens". *Jaarverslagen Vereiniging voor Terpenonderzoek* 20–24 (1940), pp. 26–115 & pl. 1–28.

Groothedde, M., "The Vikings in Zutphen (Netherlands. Military organisation and early town development after the Vikingraid in 882". In: R. Simek & U. Engel (eds), *Vikings on the Rhine. Recent Research on Early Medieval Relations between the Rhinelands and Scandinavia* (Vienna 2004), pp. 111–132.

Haertle, C.M. *Karolingische Münzfunde aus dem 9. Jahrhundert* (Cologne, Weimar and Vienna 1997).

Heeringen, R.M. van, "Een Zilveren toiletgarnituur uit de Vikingtijd van het strand van Domburg". *Walacria, een kroniek van Wlacheren* 3 (1990), pp. 51–60.

Heeringen, R.M. van, P.A. Henderikx & A. Mars (eds), *Vroeg-Middeleeuwse ringwalburgen in Zeeland* (Amersfoort 1995).

Heidinga, H.A., *Frisia in the first Millennium* (Utrecht 1997).

Henderikx, P.A., "De ringwalburgen in het mondingsgebied van de Schelde in historisch perspectief". In: R.M. van Heeringen et al. (eds), *Vroeg-Middeleeuwse ringwalburgen in Zeeland* (Amersfoort 1995), pp. 71–112.

Hermann, B. & H. Rötting, "Ein Leichenschatten mit besonderer Aussagemöglichkeit". *Archäologisches Korrespondenzblatt* 13 (1983), pp. 499–502.

Knol, E., *De Noordnederlandse kustlanden in de vroege middeleeuwen*. Ph.D. thesis, Vrije Universiteit Amsterdam (Groningen 1993).

— "Carolingian weapons from the Northern Netherlands, particularly from the cemetery of Godlinze". In: B. Arrhenius (ed.), *Kingdoms and Regionality, Transactions from the 49th Sachsersymposium 1998 in Uppsala*. Theses and Papers in Archaeology B 6 (2001), pp. 115–120.

— "Gold und Silber aus Marsum – karolingische Schatzfunde in den Niederlande". In: E. Wamers & M. Brandt (eds), *Die Macht des Silbers, Karolingsiche Schätze im Norden* (Regensburg 2005), pp. 119–124.

— "Kauri's in Wierdenland". *Stad en Lande* 15.1 (2006), pp. 6–7.

— "Het Karolingische grafveld De bouwerd bij Ezinge (Gr.)". *Verslagen van de Vereniging voor Terpenonderzoek*. pp. 83–90 (2007), pp. 62–89.

Knol, E. & J.H. Looijenga, "A Tau Staff with Inscriptions from Bernsterburen (Friesland)". In: R.H. Bremmer, G. Van der Meer & O. Vries (eds), *Aspects of Old Frisian Philology*. Amsterdamer Beitäge zur älteren Germanistik, 31/32 (Amsterdam and Groningen 1990), pp. 226–241.

Knol, E., W. Prummel, H.T. Uytterschaut, M.L.P. Hoogland, W.A. Casparie, G.J. de Langen, E. Kramer & J. Schelvis, "The early medieval cemetery of Oosterbeintum (Frl)". *Palaeohistoria* 37/38 (1996), pp. 245–416.

Knol, E. & X. Bardet, "Carolingian weapons from the Cemetery of Godlinze, the Netherlands". In: H. Sarfatij et al. (eds), *In Discussion with the Past. Archaeological Studies Presented to W.A. van Es* (Zwolle 1999), pp. 213–223.

Laux, F., "Uberlegungen zum Reihengräberfriedhof von Ashausen, Gem. Stelle, Kreis Harburg (Niedersachsen)". *Studien zur Sachsenforschung* 6 (Neumünster 1987), pp. 123–154.

Miedema, M., *Vijfentwintig eeuwen bewoning in het terpenland ten noordwesten van Groningen*. Ph.D. thesis, Vrije Universiteit Amsterdam (Dieren 1983).

— "Het archeologisch materiaal uit de terp Wierhuizen". *Groningsche Volksalmanak* (1989), pp. 76–164.

— "Oost-Fivelingo 250 v.Chr. – 1850 n. Chr. (archeologische kartering en beschrijving van 200 jaar bewoning in noordoost Groningen)". *Palaeohistoria* 32 (1990), pp. 111–245.

Nikolay, J., "Een politiek machtscentrum in noordelijk Westergo, goudvondsten uit het Fries-Groningse terpengebied, 450–650". In: E. Kramer et al. (eds), *Koningen van de Noordzee* (2003), pp. 55–74.

— "Nieuwe bewonders van het terpengebied en hun rol bij de opkomst van het Friese koningsschap. De betekenis van gouden bracteaten en bracteaatachtige hangers uit Friesland (vijfde-zevende eeuw na. Chr.)". *De Vrije Fries* 85 (2005), pp. 37–103.

Pol, A., "Spectaculaire schatvondst uit de 9e eeuw". *De Beeldenaar* 16 (2) (1992), pp. 66–71.

Roes, A., *Bone and antler objects from the Frisian terp-mounds* (Haarlem 1963).

Simek, R. & U. Engels (eds), *Vikings on the Rhine, Recent Research on Early Medieval Relations between the Rhinelands and Scandinavia* (Wien Fassvaender 2004).

Taayke, E., *Die einheimische Keramik der nördlichen Niederlande, 600 v.Chr. bis 300 n. Chr.* Ph.D. thesis, Groningen (also *Berichten Rijksdienst Oudheidkundig Bodemonderzoek* 40 (1990): pp. 101–222; 41 (1995): 9–102; 42 (1996): 9–208) (1996).

Tempel, W.-D., *Die Dreilagenkämme aus Haithabu, Studien zu den Kämmen der Wikingerzeit im Nordseeküstengebiet und Skandinavien*. Dissertation (Göttingen 1969).

Theuws, F., "Grave goods, ethnicity, and the rhetoric of burial rites in Late Antique Northern Gaul". In: T. Derks & N. Roymans (eds), *Ethnic Constructs in Antiquity* (Amsterdam 2009), pp. 283–319.

Vos, P.C. & R.M. van Heeringen, *Holocene Geology and Occupation History of the Province of Zeeland* (= Mededelingen Nederlands Instituut voor toegepaste geowetenschappen) TNO 59 (1997).

Waterbolk, H.J. & H.T. Waterbolk, "Amber of the coast of the Netherlands". In: H. Thoen et al. (eds), *Studia Archaeologica Liber Amicorum Jacques A.E. Nenquin* (1991), pp. 201–209.

Westphal. H., "Franken order Sachsen? Untersuchungen an frühmittelalterichen Waffen". *Studien zur Sachsenforschung* 14 (2002), pp. 1–310.

Willemsen, A. *Vikings! Raids in the Rhine/Meuse Region 800–1000* (Utrecht 2004).

Woltering, P.J., "The Archaeology of Texel". Ph.D. thesis, Vrije Universiteit Amsterdam (also *Berichten Rijksdienst Oudheidkundig Bodemonderzoek* 25 (1975): pp. 7–36; 29 (1979): 7–113; 42 (1996): 209–363; 44 (2001): 9–396) (2000).

Woltering, P.J., J.C. Besteman, J.F. van Regteren Altena & D.P. Hallewas, "Early Medieval North Holland Surveyed, the Hollands Noorderkwartier Sheet: Early Middle Ages of the Archaeological Map of the Netherlands". *Berichten van de*

Rijkdienst voor het Oudheidkundig Bodemonderzoek 43 (1999), pp. 361–370.

Woltering, P.J., "Vroeg-middeleeuws Den Burg op Texel. Een versterkte nederzetting uit de 7e–8e eeuw". In: P.J. Woltering, W.J.H. Verwers & G.H. Scheepstra (eds), *Middleeuwse toestanden, Archeologie, geschiedenis en monumentenzorg* (Hilversum 2002), pp. 25–57.

W.J.H. Verwers

Vikings in the lower Rhine area?

Introduction

In this article I shall attempt to establish evidence of the presence of the Vikings in the Lower Rhine area. I shall focus on the area in the centre of the Netherlands, between the rivers Rhine, Lek, Kromme Rijn, Waal and Meuse. These rivers played an important role in the development of this area because they formed the main waterways in the central part of the Netherlands and connected several parts of Western Europe with each other. Within this framework an important role was played by the trade centres of Dorestad and Tiel, fig. 1.

Fig. 1. Situation, central river area, Dorestad and Tiel.

The Kromme Rijn area, between Utrecht in the north and Wijk bij Duurstede in the south, was controlled by a local elite during the 5th century whose power was based on the ownership of land. This elite maintained contact with the Frankish people in Austrasia. There, between the middle Rhine and the upper Meuse area, the Merovingians established a state in the 6th century which originally, about a century earlier, was situated around Paris.

Excavations in De Geer, a new housing estate northwest of Wijk bij Duurstede, discovered the presence of the local elite habitation. An indication of the relatively high status of the local people is shown by a hoard consisting of three gold coins of Justinian dated to 570 and a number of fragments of the objects. These finds strongly indicate the existence of international or interregional relations of the people in De Geer. It is unclear how these objects reached De Geer: either by trade or by exchange of gifts. In any case, the Franks must have been responsible for the transport of these gold objects.

An initiative for the contacts with the local elite would have been taken by the Frankish nobility in the hope to win the regional elite of the river area to their side. The Frankish diplomatic activities must have been fairly succesful, because we know of the foundation of a church in the Roman military fort of Utrecht in 630 by the Merovingian king Dagobert. The second positive indication is the move of the mintmaster Madelinus from Maastricht to Dorestad, which took place at the same time. Madelinus is considered to be the exponent of the Frankish expansion in the first half of the 7th century. In fact, the Madelinus triens, minted in Dorestad, as the reverse shows, is the oldest numismatical evidence of the existence of Dorestad.

The Frankish influence was not, however, solidly rooted, because the Frisians living along the coast in the west and the north of the Netherlands destroyed the above mentioned church soon after its construction. Trade activities brought the Frisians into contact with the central river area. In fact the Franks had a similar interest and the central river area formed a border between the Frisians and the Franks, especially during the 7th century. Several battles had been fought, but the final victory went to the Franks around 720. From that moment the Frisian area, including the Kromme Rijn area, was ultimately incorporated into the Frankish empire. Although Dorestad had existed as an *emporium* for more than a century its period of prosperity started from that date. The result was population growth, eco-

W.J.H. Verwers

nomic expansion and, finally, the establishment of Dorestad as an international trade centre.

The dating of Dorestad as trade centre is based on historical, numismatical, dendrochronological and C14 data. Inside Dorestad, habitation features from the first half of the 7th century, when Madelinus was active there, are lacking, except in De Geer. The earliest traces of Dorestad can be ascribed to the middle of that century. Tree-ring analysis of the wooden wells, consisting mostly of imported barrels, of which hundreds were found, give datings between 691 and 837. Pottery presents a similar dating: from after the middle of the 7th to the second half of the 9th century. The local coinage ended about 830. Coins minted elsewhere show a peak of activity between 775 and 825.

After the middle of the 9th century the settlement declined and Dorestad lost its function as an international trade centre. There are several reasons for the "end" of Dorestad. The process of shifting and silting up of the riverbed of the Kromme Rijn must be mentioned in the first place. Furthermore, we would like to mention the political instability in the Carolingian Empire, which provided an opportunity for the Vikings to attack the region.

Dorestad's role as an international trade centre remains in the foreground. An immense quantity of wheel-turned pottery imported from the German Rhine area near Badorf and Mayen, for instance, points to this function, which was taken over in the second half of the 9th century by Tiel, as we know from historical sources. Tiel was mentioned for the first time in these sources about 855. This trade centre preserved its function as a transhipment harbour until the 12th century.

Dorestad

Dorestad was situated near the bifurcation of the rivers Lower Rijn/Lek and the Kromme Rijn. The Lower Rijn formed a direct link with the German Rijn area. The Kromme Rijn provided connections to the routes to England, the northern part of the Netherlands, North Germany and Scandinavia. Via Lek, the Scheldt and Meuse delta could be reached. To the south a watercourse between Zoelen and Zoelmond, today gone, gave access to the middle and upper Meuse area.

The Kromme Rijn cut through a zone of fossil stream-ridges which

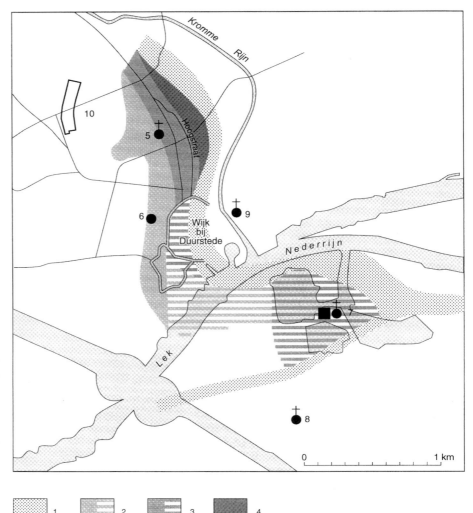

Fig. 2. Schematic reconstruction of Dorestad. Legend: 1 course of (Kromme) Rijn and Lek during the Carolingian period; 2 agrarian zone; 3 commercial area; 4 foreshore Noorderwijk; 5 cemetery and church (?) De Heul; 6 cemetery De Engk; 7 cemetery and church in Roman castellum Levefanum; 8 church of Rijswijk; 9 church of Leur; 10 De Geer.

were relatively high and dry. On these ridges inhabitants of Dorestad built their houses and they used this area for agriculture and stockbreeding. Basins, probably permanently under water, lay beyond these ridges. The edges of the basins were suitable for natural pastureland.

As far as we know, Dorestad consisted of three parts: the northern river area on either side of the Hoogstraat, situated on one of the ridges, the *castellum* district in the south and the middle zone in between, fig. 2.

The situation in the south, where the Kromme Rijn branched off

W.J.H. Verwers

from the Lower Rhine and the Lek, is hypothetical because of the post-Carolingian time activity of the rivers that has destroyed all archaeological traces. For this reason excavations were pointless there. Although the exact location is unknown, we can assume that the Roman Limes *castellum* Levefanum, indicated on the *Tabula Peutingeriana*, a copy of a 3rd-century Roman map, stood there. A second indication for the position of the *castellum* was the character of the dredged finds, found during sand extractions from the riverbed of the Rhine, including Roman pottery and a Roman military helmet. The Merovingian and Carolingian pottery sherds combined with the presence of the Roman fort led to the supposition, based on similar situations in military forts along the Roman frontier zone, that Dorestad was developed in and around this Roman fort. It must have been an attractive place for the Merovingian elite to settle. They identified themselves as successors to the Roman Empire. The *castellum* district consisted of at least two parts: the castellum and the vicus with the harbour. The clergy and the king's representatives would probably have lived in the Roman fort. The workshop of mintmaster Madelinus was also established here. This castellum district had its own cemetery, as shown by the dredged human bone material.

Further to the north, in the middle of Dorestad, the situation is more obvious. This part of Dorestad, with its own cemetery on De Engk, was about 600 m in length and situated west of the late-medieval town centre of Wijk bij Duurstede. This part was about 100 m wide. Directly south of the Hoogstraat, the Kromme Rijn eroded its left bank, probably at the end of the Carolingian period or even later. Because it is assumed that erosion has destroyed a zone of at most 100 m, the settlement may have been 200 m wide here. Only a small part has been excavated. As far as we know, this part or, at any rate, the most western side of this part must have had an agrarian function.

The excavation of Dorestad

Between 1967 and 1977 vast archaeological effort was concentrated in the northern district of Dorestad, directly north of the present town Wijk bij Duurstede. The excavations were carried out by the Rijksdienst voor Oudheidkundig Bodemonderzoek (ROB, State Service for Archaeological Investigations) under the direction of Prof. Dr. W.A. van Es.

In the 7th century the left bank of the Kromme Rijn had been immediately east of the Hoogstraat, which means High Street. In the 8th century the Kromme Rijn began to move eastwards. This resulted in a meander opposite the site of Dorestad. At the end of Dorestad's heyday the distance between the Hoogstraat and the middle of the bend had increased to 200 m. This natural development came to an end in the 12th century. This situation has remained unchanged up to the present. How the inhabitants of Dorestad reacted to the result of the natural shifting of the river into an eastern direction and how they used this area will be discussed later.

West of the riverbank along the Hoogstraat a 3 m wide road ran along the embankment from north to south. On the western side of the road the front houses of the *vicus* were built. The houses stood on parcels with their longitudinal axis towards the river. Because of the present overbuilding, the pattern of this part of the settlement is not clear. Only in the north of this district were several houseplans, bordering to the riverbank area, excavated. The rectangular houses, with entrances in the long sides, and measuring about 15 × 6 m, were situated on their own yards, fig. 3. As far as we know, the *vicus* consisted of three or more rows of houses parallel to the river.

In the rear part of the *vicus*, opposite the widest part of the meander of the river, the people of Dorestad buried their dead in the cemetery of De Heul. The cemetery can be divided into several parts. In the middle of the largest part of the cemetery a rectangular wooden building of about 15 × 8 m was constructed. Its position and shape indicate that the building must have had a special function, probably as a church. A minimum number of individuals buried in west-east oriented graves, is assumed to be about 2350.

Behind this cemetery and north and south of it there was a zone with large wooden buildings on enclosed rectangular plots. The distribution of these buildings in this part is less dense than in the *vicus*. The houses are of the boat-shaped type with long, slightly curved walls. One of them, with inclined outer piles, has been reconstructed in De Schothorst estate in the north of Amersfoort, fig. 4. The interior was divided into two sections of unequal length by two entrances in the long sides, opposite each other. The longest section is thought to be a byre, the smaller part the living section. In the short sides of each section there was a door. The length of these buildings varied between 20 and 30 m, the width between 6–8 m, fig. 5. Granaries were often found outside. Therefore, these houses are thought to

W.J.H. Verwers

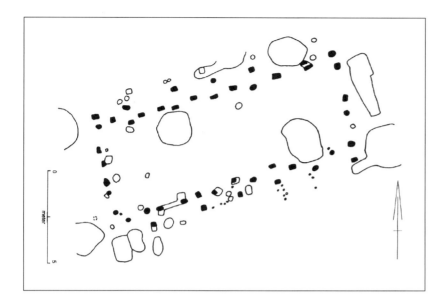

Fig. 3. Dorestad, house plan. Scale 1:200.

Fig. 4. Amersfoort, Schothorst, reconstruction of a Dorestad house.

Vikings in the lower Rhine area?

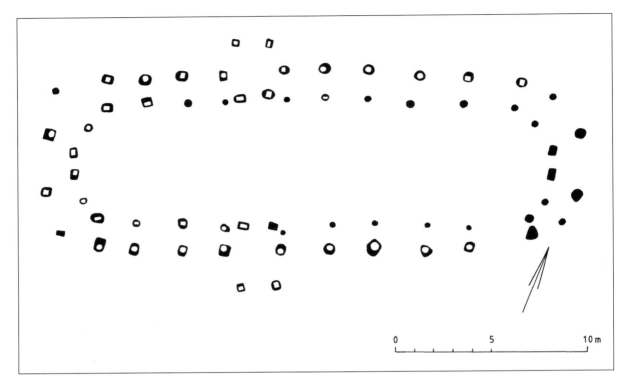

Fig. 5. Dorestad, house plan.

be farms, thus this part of the settlement had an agrarian function. Future research must provide an answer to the question whether these more or less isolated farms belonged to inhabitants with a relatively high status or whether they represent a young phase in the development of the settlement or a combination of both.

Roads ran through this part of the settlement. Rows of postholes, indicating wooden causeways, were found between the riverbank area and De Heul cemetery. Although the details are obscure, the roads ran parallel or at right angles to the riverbank area.

Dorestad's riverbank area

Now I shall return to the riverbank area, east of the Carolingian road, which formed a border to the *vicus* and ran more or less parallel to the present

W.J.H. Verwers

Hoogstraat. East of the Hoogstraat we have carried out five excavations in the riverbank area, called Hoogstraat 0–IV.

The eastward shift of the river led to the accretion of new land in the concave bend of the river. Especially during wintertime this area was wet because it is situated relatively low. Numerous finds and thousands of posts show that this area was used intensively by the people of Dorestad. From east to west the length of the wooden constructions is 200 m. After an analysis of the schematised plan, we can conclude that the river bank was divided into parcels of more or less equal width – about 9 m. Parcels often occurred in pairs and formed a continuation of the division inside the *vicus* on the other side of the Carolingian road. Between these parcels, strips of 2–4 m width were used for soil-extraction to fill the timber-earth causeways. The outside of these causeways consisted of wicker revetments.

Construction of the causeways was completed in a continuous process in a number of phases. Probably a new segment was added every year. The expansion of the waterfront structures did not take place at the same time, and this resulted in the development of an indented, not a closed riverfront. In the final phase, the central part of the curve of this riverbank complex had grown to 200 m in length.

In the development of the bank constructions two phases were recognised, fig. 6 (the division in the middle of the figure). The first one started after the middle of the 7th century, the second at least two generations later, about 720, when Dorestad definitively came into the hands of the Franks.

One of the problems is whether the erection of the constructions in the riverbank area started over the total length or on individual spots along the Hoogstraat. Was the local elite living in De Geer responsible for the building activities? Another question is whether the habitation was equally intensive along the southern Hoogstraat. In any case, the northern Hoogstraat excavations give the impression that the riverbank was abandoned earlier than in the southern Hoogstraat excavations. This presents a contrast to the situation southwards. In the Hoogstraat III area and the zone west of it, habitation continued without interruption until the 12th century, but was limited.

The present opinion, in contrast to what was said in the Hoogstraat I publication, is that these bank constructions were built-over. The posts in the centre of the constructions represent the lower part of wooden buildings. Initial platforms, solid constructions of about 12 m², were built against

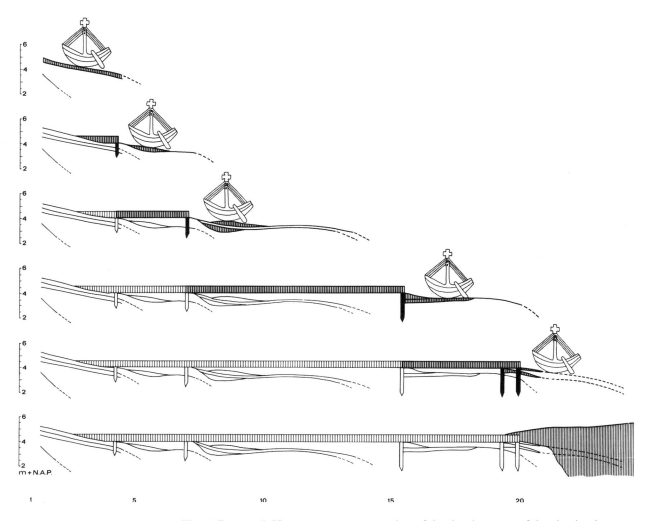

Fig. 6. Dorestad, Hoogstraat, reconstruction of the development of the riverbank complex (without wooden buildings).

the bank. They marked a start of the building activity of the riverbank. On these platforms were built small constructions comparable with granaries or *Speicher*. Later, about 100 m away from the original bank near the Hoogstraat, a second row was formed. These constructions may have been

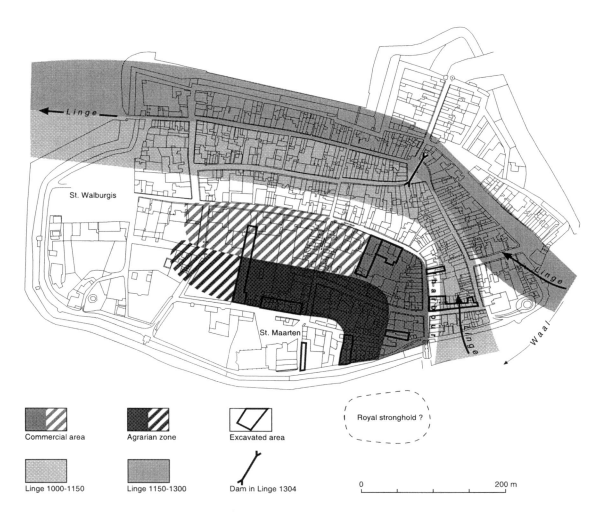

Fig. 7. Tiel, town centre, schematic reconstruction with presumed former courses of the Linge.

similar to the oldest ones, but it is not inconceivable that they were connected to each other so that segmented buildings developed. Comparable structures are known from several excavations, such as Dalem and Flögeln in north Germany.

Vikings in the lower Rhine area?

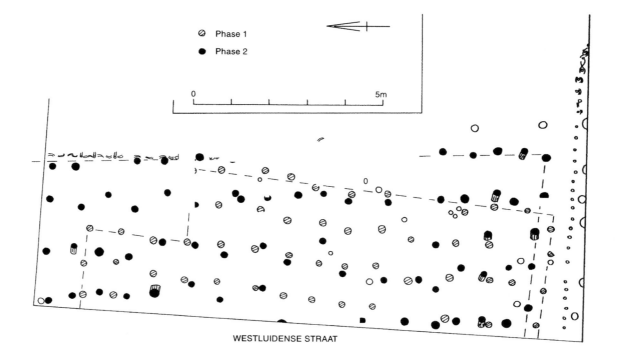

Fig. 8. Tiel-Zuid, embankment constructions phase 1–2, late 9th–11th century.

Tiel

The system of land acquisition in Dorestad is not an isolated phenomenon. Tiel, a town at the junction of the rivers Waal and Linge, took over the function of Dorestad as an international transhipment harbour after the middle of the 9th century, fig. 7. Its most prosperous period was in the second half of the 10th and the 11th century. It is beyond the scope of this article to discuss the excavations of Tiel in detail, but I would like to pay special attention to the harbour constructions, and to the constructions of the oldest phases: from the end of the 9th century until 965 and between 965–1100. Although the function is not identical to that of Dorestad, I see in Tiel a fairly similar system of wooden constructions.

After 985 the embankment was divided into parellel strips by means of fairly narrow revetted piers filled and raised with earth and oriented at right angles to the shoreline. This might indicate a type of parcelling into separately owned plots in line with the parcelling on the landside. The strips were about 5–7 m wide. The sides of the piers were strengthened with planks, mostly ship's timber.

According to those who excavated the site, the division into parcels must have been a radical change compared with the previous system. They distinguished two phases, based especially on the depth of the posts. In the first phase this system consisted of a construction of individual platforms, built on wooden piles and replaced 75 years later by a single uninterrupted quay platform which was built as a whole, fig. 8.

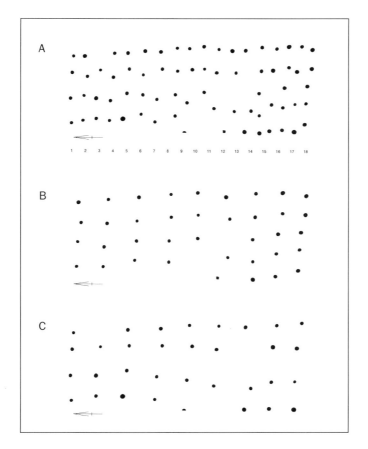

Fig. 9. Tiel-Zuid, embankment constructions phase 2: A all posts, B phase 2a, C phase 2b. Scale 1:200.

Vikings in the lower Rhine area?

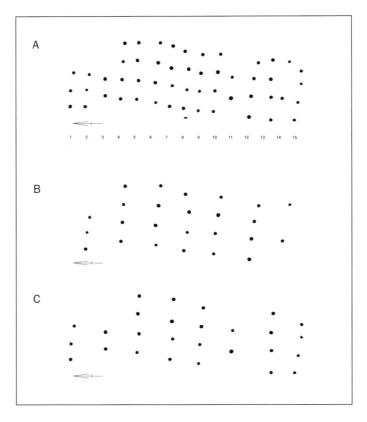

Fig. 10. Tiel-Zuid, embankment constructions phase 1: A. all posts, B. phase 1a, C. phase 1b. Scale 1:200.

Based on the plan of the second phase, I would like to point out three elements. In the north-south rows of the posts there is some difference in the depth of the posts, although they would have been driven in at the same time. Secondly, in both eastern north-south rows the posts stood in an irregular, alternating pattern. Finally, the posts are very close to each other. The distance between the posts varies in general from 60 to 90 cm, sometimes even reaching 1.60 m, fig. 9A. I therefore prefer another interpretation. The plan of phase 2 was divided into two subphases, 2a and 2b. To subphase 2a belong the posts in the even, to subphase 2b those in the odd numbered rows, fig. 9B–C. This gives us more regular plans, where the dis-

W.J.H. Verwers

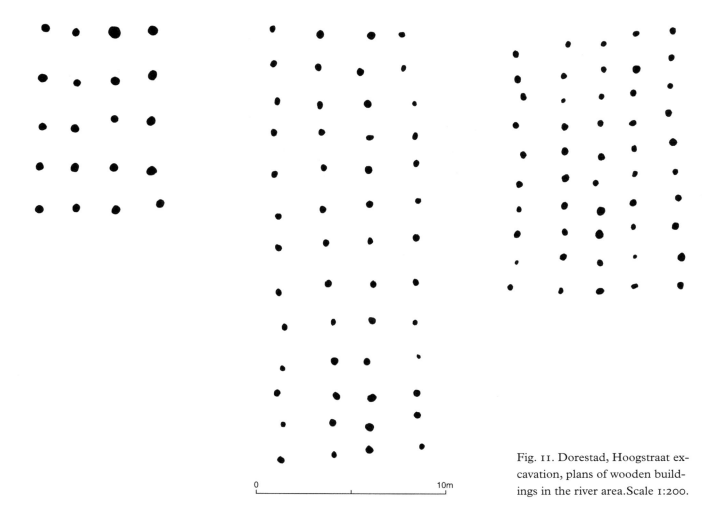

Fig. 11. Dorestad, Hoogstraat excavation, plans of wooden buildings in the river area. Scale 1:200.

tance between the posts varies in general from 1.50 to 2 m with the depth of the posts being more similar in each subphase. Likewise, the oldest phase has been split up into two subphases, fig. 10. Indicators for the dating of the subphases are absent, as is information about the width of the parcels. Probably the platforms consisted of relatively short constructions with 3 × 4, 4 × 4 or 3 × 5 piles. Piles next to these constructions may be extensions or repairs. It is unknown whether buildings stood on these platforms.

Apart from some problems regarding the details of the interpretation (such as: why were the posts of the subphases more or less equidistant from each other, was it a systematic repair?), the new created platforms in

Vikings in the lower Rhine area?

Fig. 12. Dorestad, Hoogstraat excavation, ship fragments.

Tiel are generally very similar to those of Dorestad. The constructions in Dorestad consisted of mostly four rows of at least 4 posts. This number could rise sometimes to 13 posts, fig. 11. They formed the substructures of the above-mentioned buildings. The fact that the length of the platforms in Tiel and Dorestad differs was caused by the local conditions of nature.

In my view, the plans and the system of the embankment constructions in Tiel are comparable to those of Dorestad. In fact, the building systems in Dorestad and Tiel can be assumed to be the precursors of the medieval harbour constructions of Bergen in Norway.

In Tiel the bank of the river was too steep to pull the ships ashore, which is why people built jetties. With regard to the situation in Dorestad we believe that both above mentioned landing methods were used, depending on the depth of the ships. Shallow ships could enter the ditches between

W.J.H. Verwers

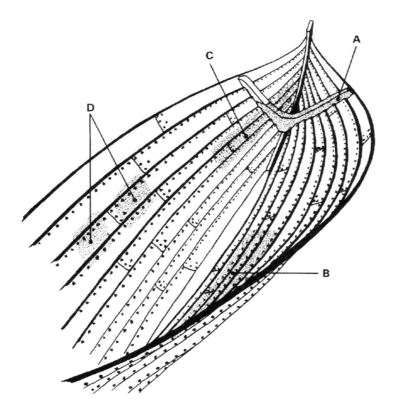

Fig. 13. Tiel-Zuid, position of ship fragments A-D, found in the Tiel excavation, indicated in a reconstructed clinker-built Viking ship.

the causeways or were pulled ashore at the end of the causeways. At high tide it was also possible for deep ships to quay there.

In Dorestad and Tiel wooden remains of ships have been found. The Hoogstraat II excavation in Dorestad revealed several fragments which lay scattered in the clay and sand deposits of the river bank area. As far as could be recognised, these fragments belonged to a clinker-built boat, fig. 12. The context of the find dates these fragments to the second half of the 8th and the first half of the 9th century.

In Tiel a part of a clinker-built ship and a V-formed floor timber were found, fig. 13. Both elements, secondarily used in the construction of the wooden revetment, were made of oak. According to dendrochronological research, the trees used for the Tiel ships came from southwest England, close to London, where they were felled between 971 and 1008. Written sources

Vikings in the lower Rhine area?

mention intensive contacts between Tiel and London at that time. Somewhat earlier, the Vikings attacked Tiel. Their last array dates from 1006.

The ships, whose wooden remains have been preserved in Dorestad and Tiel, were built in the Scandinavian shipbuilding tradition. Examples of these ships are known in Denmark and north Germany.

Viking presence in Dorestad and Tiel?

Written sources mention that the Vikings came to Dorestad for the first time in 834. Their last array, according to the sources, took place in 863. Obviously, nothing was to be got there. Consequently, the question whether the Vikings ever were in this area can be answered positively on the basis of historical sources.

The ship fragments mentioned above do not prove that the Vikings lived in the Lower Rhine area. At best they indicate contacts with the people of Dorestad and Tiel.

Finds show a similar picture. Among the dredged and stray finds, known before the beginning of the Dorestad excavation in 1967, there were swords ascribed to the Vikings. The origin of the weapons, however, could not be proved. It is known that the Vikings traded in blades of swords with Scandinavian hilts. Specialists in forging weapons were travelling through Northwest Europe at that time. One sword found in Dorestad was primarily linked with the Vikings. Research of forging techniques, however, revealed that it was a Frankish product.

Finally, I would like to mention a golden necklace and two silver needles with filigree decoration, fig. 14. The needles were discovered in Dorestad; however, Domburg, England, north Germany and Scandinavia revealed similar objects that were ascribed to the 10th century. The production was thought to have been in the hands of the Vikings. Because of the context of the find, the Dutch objects must be older. Although it cannot be proved, there probably was a local production of these needles in the Netherlands. A more or less comparable necklace from Scandinavia is also more recent than the Dorestad object. Two bracelets found in the Hoogstraat excavations point to a production in Northern Europe, but are dated to the 8th and 9th centuries.

Conclusion: the archaeological data provides clear indications of the existence of contacts between the people of Dorestad and Tiel with the

W.J.H. Verwers

Vikings in the Lower Rhine area. However, interpretation of the nature of these contacts is rather difficult, which is in contrast with the written sources. The latter, in any case, mention Vikings raids. But like the Frisians, they may also have played an important role in the trade of Western Europe.

Note

Since I wrote this paper in 1999, Prof. van Es and I have finished the research in the riverbank area. The results have been published in 2009 (W.A. van Es & W.J.H. Verwers, *Excavations at Dorestad 3, Hoogstraat 0, II–IV*, Nederlandse Oudheden 16, Amersfoort). The interpretation of the results differs to some extent from those presented here. Based on those results we have continued intensively the last years to analyse the structures of the settlement, the cemeteries, the dating of Dorestad, etc., also in relation to the the riverbank area excavations. We hope to finish our third book on the development and function of the settlement of Dorestad within a few years.

C. Jefferis (Zaandam) corrected the English text.

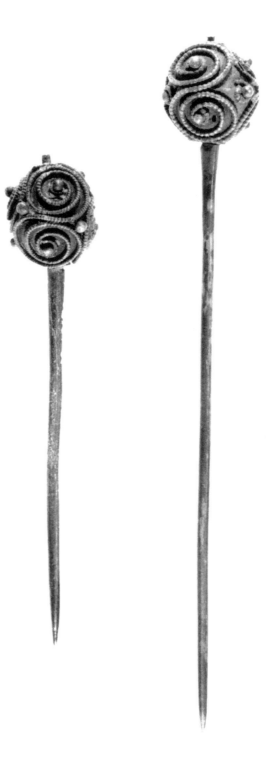

Fig. 14. Dorestad, 'Viking' finds. Photo: RMO, Leiden.

References

Dijkstra, J., *Archeologisch onderzoek in de binnenstad van Tiel; juni t/m september 1996; lokaties Koornmarkt en Tol-Zuid*. ROB Rapportages Archeologische Monumentenzorg 57 (Amersfoort 1998).

Es, W.A. van, "Dorestad Centred". In: J.C. Besteman et al. (eds), *Medieval Archaeology in the Netherlands; Studies Presented to H.H. van Regteren Altena*. Studies in Prae- en Protohistorie 4 (= ROB overdrukken, 367) (Assen and Maastricht 1990), pp. 151–182.

Es, W.A. van and W.A.M. Hessing (eds), *Romeinen, Friezen en Franken in het hart van Nederland: van Traiectum naar Dorestad (50 v.C.–950 n.C.)* (Utrecht 1994).

Es, W.A. van and W.J.H. Verwers, "Aufstieg, Blüte und Niedergang der frühmittelalterlichen Handelsmetropole Dorestad". In: K. Brandt et al. (eds), *Haithabu und die frühe Stadtentwicklung im nördlichen Europa*. Schriften des Archäologischen Landesmuseums 8 (Neumünster 2002), pp. 281–301.

— *Excavations at Dorestad 3. Hoogstraat 0, II–IV*. Nederlandse Oudheden 16 (Amersfoort 2009)

Sarfatij, H., "Tiel in succession to Dorestad". In: H. Sarfatij et al. (eds), *In Discussion with the Past. Archaeological Studies Presented to W.A. van Es* (Zwolle and Amersfoort 1999), pp. 267–278.

W.J.H. Verwers

Laurent Mazet-Harhoff

The incursion of the Vikings into the natural and cultural landscape of upper Normandy

Introduction

The Viking period of the coastal and river areas of Upper Normandy is not very well known because of the lack of material culture remains from the so-called "Scandinavian colonisation". However, written sources from the Carolingian and ducal periods – between the first Viking incursions into the Seine valley in AD 840 and the years 1010–1020 when the duchy was established – mention a number of harbours, shelled along the river.

On the basis of this information, the extent of the communication and transport networks in this period has been questioned: was the Viking colonisation a result of an early control of the sea routes and crossroads?

In order to understand the plan behind the military ports of call and other Scandinavian settlements in Upper Normandy, it is important to examine the ancient network of roads and to reconstruct the ancient river landscape of the Seine. This way it is possible to reveal the conditions for the navigation of Viking ships – whose manoeuvrability is well known in Scandinavia – and thus identify the factors behind the incursion of the Viking hordes into Frankish territory. The cognitive background of the Scandinavian seamen or navigators, whose control over Normandy is reflected in a network of toponyms of Scandinavian origin, will also be taken into account.

By examining the old communication networks of Upper Normandy through the eyes of a Scandinavian seaman, we will try to assess the Viking contribution to the territorial control of the future duchy, reflected in transport and new roads, which, however, remains to be analysed archaeologically.

*

The main characteristics of the Viking period in the lower Seine area of ancient Neustria is the mobility of its main actors: the Vikings, their victims and the Frankish defence. Both historians and archaeologists, therefore, have a shared difficulty in tracing the former Scandinavians in the modern territory of Upper Normandy in the period from the first Viking raids into the Seine valley in AD 841 and until the establishment of the Norman Duchy in 1010–1020, when this area re-established its Continental identity. Central to this question is the possibility of transport and communication. How did the Vikings travel through the ancient landscape? And would the presence of the Vikings leave any archaeologically identifiable traces of early settlements in the cultural landscape? Would the archaeological remains on their own be enough to identify traces of the colonisation that led to the development of the Norman Duchy? Before discussing these questions through an analysis of the cultural landscape of Upper Normandy, the state of research has to be outlined in order to define key issues for the Viking settlements in Upper Normandy and in the lower Seine valley in particular.

The Viking progress from raids to colonisation: research history, key issues and research strategy

Up until now the lack of archaeological evidence of the Vikings in France has made any investigation based only on material culture difficult. This is in contrast to the numerous linguistic and written sources on which a large number of publications, generally discussing the Vikings in their home countries, are based.

Worth mentioning are Jules Lair[1] and Ferdinand Lot,[2] who at the turn of the 20th century made the first historiography of the Carolingian documents mentioning Viking activities in the Seine valley. In their opinion the Vikings played a significant role in the development of the Carolingian society towards feudality, but they did not assess the impact on the local area. Lucien Musset,[3] on the other hand, focused on causalities and he discussed the Scandinavian presence on basis of a precise analysis of the written sources and the toponyms. However, the Viking period was always discussed from a Continental point of view and never within an archaeological and maritime framework that might have revealed the logistic and structural aspects of the occupation, an aspect common for Viking settlements in north-western Europe.

In his last work, *Les invasions normandes, une catastrophe?*, the Belgian historian Albert d'Haenens[4] in 1970 recommended a range of archaeological projects, specific to invasion as a phenomenon and illustrated by the

Vikings on the Continent. Since then several new analyses have been presented, but often restricted to their respective disciplinary areas.

Very few studies discussing the geographical distribution of the Scandinavian settlements also include the toponymic evidence. Gillian Fellows-Jensen,[5] however, presented comparative research of both English and Norman toponyms, thus adding a new perspective to a territorial approach to the Viking occupation. On both sides of the Channel the toponyms of Scandinavian origin comprise place-names whose structural and etymological mixtures show both a cognitive adaptation of the immigrants to the local cultural landscapes and also show migration between Scandinavian colonies.

The archaeological contributions are limited to some articles, of which the oldest were written before the expansion of rescue excavations, and the authors tried enthusiastically to associate some finds with the Viking occupation such as the rampart of the Le Hague dike and the controversial burials at Réville in Cotentin. Concerning the boat grave found at Île de Groix south of Brittany,[6] the German archaeologist Michael Müller-Wille in the 1970s tried to place the weapons found there in a North-European context.[7]

In an otherwise remarkable paper Birgitta Elmquist[8] discussed the unique oval brooches from Pîtres in Upper Normandy, which are associated with the Scandinavian presence in the Seine area. Her examination of the archaeological evidence of this find, which was discovered several decades ago, but with no records of the stratigraphic context, did not succeed in giving better documentation of the ethnic and demographic origins of Normandy.

More recently one of the broadest but most thorough contributions on the Vikings in France, and Brittany in particular, was published by Neil S. Price,[9] who suggested that the boat grave on Île de Groix was no isolated case, and that a search for this type of territorial monument would result in locating Scandinavian settlements.

Of other relevant works, an article on the Scandinavian weapon finds of the Seine valley by Patrick Périn[10] ought to be mentioned. The author wisely refrains from further conclusions, and it has to be admitted that only metallographic analysis of these isolated objects could distinguish Carolingian artefacts from Scandinavian products of similar shape.

Jacques Le Maho,[11] a specialist on Medieval Upper Normandy and the history of Rouen, pleads for a more indirect search for the Viking presence, attaching importance to the disruption and continuity between the Frankish and ducal periods in Normandy. The results of his excavations around the cathedral of Rouen indicate a reorganisation of the ancient city under the first dukes, but they produced no proper Scandinavian evidence. That said, it appears necessary for him to connect the city with the lower valley as a monastic *portus*.

In spite of the extent of rescue excavations in the last fifteen years, following the planning of motorways and urban constructions, the imbalance between representativity in archaeological surveys in urban environment and in rural zones incites to treat the colonisation and integration process of the Vikings at a more regional level.

As it has appeared from the different investigations carried out in Normandy, the term "Viking", used within the framework of my research, amply deserves to be enlightened. It is indeed advisable to make a definition that enables us to distinguish the Vikings from the Scandinavians; but in a French-speaking historiographic context also to be able to distinguish the so-called Norman invaders (*Normanni*) – when they are not called Danes (*Dani*) or Pagans (*Pagani*) – from the Norman sedentary subjects of the new-founded principality. From a historiographic point of view this confusion has largely contributed to the integration of the Vikings into the Frankish world, perhaps more quickly than they actually were integrated.

Beyond the description of the episodic or seasonal maritime expeditions, as the initial raids of the Scandinavian warriors were, we will retain the Norse expression *fara i víkingu*, which stresses the idea of movement from one context towards another as well as the idea of a sailing community with its own identity. Thus, all the Scandinavians could not be called Vikings, just as not all Vikings had their origins in Scandinavia. In Normandy the presence of Anglo-Scandinavian place-names in the Caux area and of Hiberno-Norwegian toponyms in Cotentin suggests a cosmopolitan identity of the ships' crews which established themselves in these areas.

Whatever its connotation and the goals which were associated with it – piracy, initiatory raids, commercial or royal expeditions, or colonial conquests – we will retain the term Viking. Its dynamic maritime character connects Scandinavia to the Continent without disregarding the British Isles,

Laurent Mazet-Harhoff

also exposed to Scandinavian attacks; England as an *alter ego* for Normandy shows plenty of comparative data.

By applying the concept "maritime cultural landscape" we would like to underline the interpretation that the Viking peasant-warriors were also seamen, whose maritime culture originated from their homelands.[12] The recent investigations of the coastal structures and harbours of Denmark made it possible to reconstruct parts of the transport and communication networks which characterised the Scandinavian societies of that period.[13] At the same time, the study of these geographical connections, according to the technical capacity of the used means of transport adapted to their environment, has revealed a range of factors behind establishing transit sites[14] which articulated these geographical transport zones on a local or even regional scale.[15] Furthermore, the archaeological identification of coastal sites has made it possible to view the occupations of the hinterland in a new light.[16] In an analysis of the archaeological remains of the Scandinavian settlements in Normandy it is, therefore, important to take into account the cultural background, the "mental map", according to which maritime experience made it possible to handle new strategic situations. Viking ships are often considered as mobile camps by many historians,[17] but the use of these ships in the Norman occupation cannot justify the lack of structures connected to the Scandinavian presence in the Seine valley, although evidence of this is quoted several times in contemporary written sources between AD 841 and the first quarter of the 11th century.

The Seine River, mentioned by Carolingian written sources as a favourite route for the Viking penetration into Frankish territory, obviously played a predominant role in the settlement process taking place on its banks, if one is to believe the quotation by Hincmar of Rheims in *Annales Bertiniani* for the year 861: "The approaching winter prevented them [the Danes] from taking to the sea; instead they were distributed according to their crews in each port from this place to Paris".[18]

In order to identify the significant stages of the Scandinavian invasion and thus be able to assess the archaeological potential of the river zone, it is necessary to break down the period. Lucien Musset divided the process of colonisation into three stages: 1) a phase of recognition from 810 to 845; 2) a military phase until 911; 3) and then a political phase. We want, however,

The incursion of the Vikings into the natural and cultural landscape

to break down the progression of the Vikings in a broad sense in order to be able to evaluate the archaeological potential.

A first phase of penetration into the territory of Upper Normandy consisted of the meeting of Viking ships and their crews with the river landscape of the lower Seine. By reconstructing the ancient river morphology we should be able to reveal the nautical conditions and the logistics and structural implications with which the Vikings were confronted during their approach; therefore an archaeological reading of the Carolingian written sources is essential. Beyond the navigable waterways, the coastal and bordering interface remains to be taken into account and here another area of progression opens: the road network.

In addition to the mapped movements, the concept of invasion can also express the cultural projection of the Vikings as an ethnic group onto an already populated territory. This second phase of settlement in a broad sense covers the military actions and strategic confrontations, possibly illustrated by the numerous weapons which have been found in the river bed. The appearance of fortified sites as well as the settlements with structures such as pits, burials, wells, etc., may reveal important features of cultural contrasts.

Finally, for lack of directly identifiable Scandinavian structures, we will try to assess the contribution of the Vikings to the development of Carolingian Neustria. In this last phase of integration we will try to evaluate the cultural impact of the Vikings on the regional developments already in progress on the social, economical and political levels, such as the later urban development and the commercial progress shown in Normandy around AD 1000.

The Phase of Invasion and the Identification of the territory: The Viking raids along the Seine River according to the written evidence

The Frankish area that is intersected by the rivers Somme and Seine was, according to the written sources, the most favoured by the Vikings, who occupied the area for nearly fifty years. The river valleys were the preferred routes into the area. The Alabaster Coast and the Seine, whose reach up to Paris had been used since the first raids in AD 820, channelled most of the raids into Carolingian Francia.

In June 841 the Vikings had raided every abbey of the lower river valley: Pentale close to La Roque, the convent of Logium (former latin name of Caudebec-en-Caux), Saint-Wandrille, Jumièges and Saint-Denis in Duclair. With each new raid the economic centres of Rouen and Paris (AD 841), Beauvais (AD 850) and Amiens (AD 855) were ransomed repeatedly either for the Scandinavians' mercy or their departure. Tribute was paid successively from 861 and onwards, the so-called *Danegeld*, which consisted of up to several thousand pounds of silver, sometimes gold, supplemented by corn and cattle. These mixed ransoms – causing immediate difficulties for the Franks – yielding regular money supplies could most probably fulfil the logistic requirements of the Viking armies.

From 855 the raids were organised in fleets of several thousands of men, who took part in the "great Norman invasion" and occupied the Seine area for nearly seven years. These massive invasions which besieged Paris several times, although in vain, required military bases, which still remain to be rediscovered in several places along the River Seine and on its tributaries, and which are mentioned repeatedly in the *Annales Bertiniani*, written between AD 830 and 882.

In 885 the Vikings probably established a camp opposite Rouen on the left bank of the River Seine or on the Morin Island, now part of the right bank but out of archaeological reach. On the island of *Oscellus*, which has been identified as Oissel south of Rouen, the Vikings installed a camp fortified from 858, but besieged in vain by King Charles the Bald (843–877†) and then taken back by the Viking Weland in return for payment from the Frankish sovereign in 861.[19] A Viking fleet came up to the confluence of the Rivers Eure and Andelle (*Tellas*) close to Pîtres (*Pistis*), a strategic site[20] that Charles the Bald secured by a blockade across the river in AD 862,[21] in order to detain the invaders, but in vain. This area was occupied by the Vikings, who stayed there until AD 865. In the same area, close to Les Damps, Rollo himself may have built a horseshoe-shaped fortification in AD 900, still visible at the time of Dudo of Saint Quentin (1015–1026) and Guillaume de Jumièges (1028–1070).[22] Hincmar of Rheims in the year AD 862 writes about a repair yard for Viking ships between St Wandrille and Jumièges to which the fleets returned in 866.[23] Finally, on Jeufosse (*Fossa Givaldi*) a fortification may have been in use from AD 856 until after AD 911 and controlled the confluence of the River Epte,[24] which today still separates Normandy from Île-de-France.

Reconstruction of the ancient river landscape of the lower Seine area

How did the Seine appear to Scandinavian seamen more than a thousand years ago? Was it really such an easy nautical way that led the Vikings towards the Frankish treasures, as it is said in the Carolingian chronicles, describing surprise attacks possible because of exceptional capability of the ships?

A reconstruction of the courses and navigability of the ancient rivers depends on the following principle: each change of the river course or estuary is important for navigation as well as for anchoring and landing because of particular hydro-climatic, cyclic or tidal conditions, often combined with topographical obstacles (see fig. 1). The history of the changes of the river thus makes it possible to identify the stretches which originally were difficult to navigate and, therefore, had to be modified by human intervention. Likewise, there are three ways of long term reading of the ancient river landscape that have allowed us to identify the general morphology of the Lower Seine at the beginning of the Viking Age.

a) A retrospective examination covering the last thousand years on the basis of old charts, maps and maritime documents from the end of the Middle Ages, Renaissance and modern times,[25] highlighted permanent topographic obstacles for navigation since the Viking Age such as banks and shallows that even numerous dredging and canalizing campaigns in the 19th and 20th centuries never succeeded to erase completely.

Indeed, islands and sand banks were scattered in the estuary, which went much deeper into the inland (approximately thirty kilometres) than today. However, the silting of the estuary and the river confluences did not truly affect navigation until the end of the Middle Ages, when the phenomenon increased at the beginning of the so-called Small Ice Age.[26]

The numerous banks and islands between the estuary and Rouen, identified by micro-toponyms in the inland, were regularly swept by the tides, the height of which still reaches 7.50 m in the estuary. The famous *mascaret*, a two metre high tidal wave (spring tide) breaking on the river at its lowest water level, went up until La Mailleraye in 1963 making any approach dangerous, in particular in ford areas and inside the meanders where the wave broke more violently.[27]

The in- and outgoing tide allowed even heavy-draught ships to pass

Laurent Mazet-Harhoff

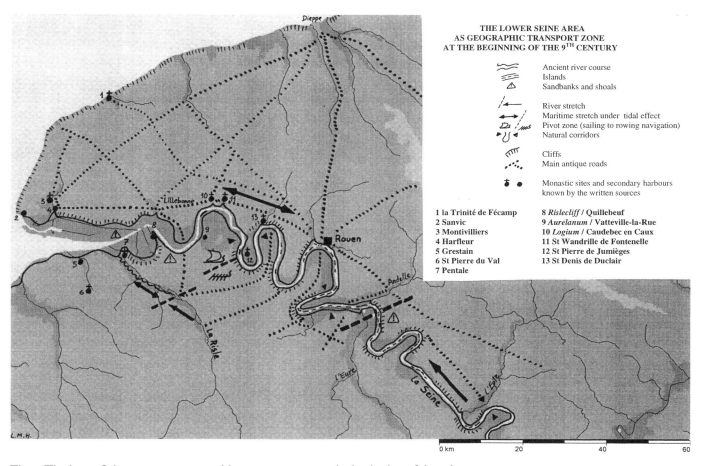

Fig. 1. The lower Seine area as a geographic transport zone at the beginning of the 9th century.

the shallow waters and to reach Rouen and the confluence of the River Eure upstream at any time of the year. On the other hand, to navigate counter current to the lock at Poses-Amfreville was much less easy during the low water season; summer was, however, the Vikings' favourite season for raiding. In order to deepen the water level on this section towards Paris many locks were in modern times installed in the shallow waters, that earlier of-

The incursion of the Vikings into the natural and cultural landscape

fered many fords to be crossed and, thus, many obstacles for the navigation. To avoid these water currents upstream from the confluence of Andelle, the digging of a canal visible on the map of Cassini from 1756 was planned in the 18th century.

b) A chronological examination of the harbours of the lower Seine valley, dated to the first millennium, emphasises constant nautical activities at the section limited upstream by the lock at Poses-Amfreville. Beyond this geological rift, we do not know of any noticeable ports from the Merovingian period. The devastating effects of the *mascaret* were already mentioned in the 7th century in *Vita et Miraculi Sancti Romani*. Later, the chroniclers of the Fontenelle abbey around 840 described the twin rivers of the Seine (*aestus Sequanae de bini*).[28] In his *De moribus et actis primorum Normanniae ducum*, Dudo of Saint Quentin also testifies to *Sequanae aesti* (the "foaming" of the river Seine),[29] which following the lunar phases went up to Jumièges. Downstream to this abbey the marshy banks were an obstacle for anchoring. Therefore, the Gallo-Romans had already established their ports in the confluent valleys, like *Juliobona* / Lillebonne, which remains the best documented port in the lower valley.[30]

c) An examination of the nautical practices adapted to river, well-documented in the 19th century before the great canalisation campaigns finally confirmed the ancient division of the river into distinct transport zones, each with its type of vessel, adapted to local nautical circumstances. Modern[31] and contemporary[32] accounts up to 1846 mention that clinker-built boats could sail up to Heurteauville *Au Bout du Vent* ("at Winds End") or to Yainville at *Claquevent*, and downstream to Jumièges, but had to continue by rowing towards Duclair.

Besides, the construction of the boats used in the 19th century is comparable with the Viking long-ships, in particular the *Bachot de Seine* with its square sail, the clinker-built *Chaloupe*, or the so-called *Norvégienne*, which Navy historians claim may not have been introduced earlier than during the 19th century by Scandinavian sailors.

It has been proved that the clinker-building technique already had strong roots in Medieval Normandy. The accounts and inventories from the shipyard of the Clos des Galées at Rouen, in activity from 1293 to 1418, distinguish very clearly in the terminology the clinker-building and local tradition from the freeboard architecture inherited from the Mediterranean tradition.[33]

Altogether, the Seine a thousand years ago may have looked like the river known at the beginning of the 19th century, whereas this differs clearly from the canalised and regulated river of today. It has to be considered that in the Viking Age the current of the river was probably equivalent with the present one. A significant morphological difference appears however: the formerly less deep river showed a broader bed to contain its water mass. Also, the variations of the water level due to the tidal effects or river cycles had a more significant influence on navigation and at the same time on the activities on its shores.

Another important factor has to be taken into account: the hydro-climatic balance of the Seine basin, which counts for much in the variations of the river flow, might influence its navigability in a much contrasted way, because of a milder but wetter climate which preceded the Small Ice Age.

Progression into the Seine valley: Navigability and logistic implications

The sea route which the Vikings followed to the estuary of the Seine had not been completely unknown to them. Since the 7th century the Friesian trade had made the Scandinavian merchants familiar with the routes crossing the Channel and the North Sea, where Frankish products (wine, weapons and textiles) met with Scandinavian waxes and furs on the monastic routes.[34]

In the limestone cliffs, stretching over 125 kilometres from Le Tréport to Cap de la Hève close to Le Havre, a few deep valleys emerge. They were controlled by ports which had been known since Antiquity: Fécamp on the river Valmont and Dieppe on the river Arques. For the Viking expeditions these coastal sites could certainly be the object of plundering. However, the trade routes that these rivers formed might appear very hazardous for armed incursions. Only their estuaries were navigable. Moreover, these well-populated zones of economic interest had been well defended since 800 at the personal command of Charlemagne.[35]

Thus, the Seine appears indeed as a favourite route for incursions. Its broad bed, from the estuary to Rouen, kept the Scandinavian crews shel-

The incursion of the Vikings into the natural and cultural landscape

tered from arrows, spears and other missiles used at that time. But, the river course was not easy to navigate.

Thanks to scientifically based sailing experiments, which have been carried out in Scandinavia, we now know more about the manoeuvrability of the Viking ships.[36] However, these warships, among which the Gokstad type remains the closest parallel to those used in Western waters in the 9th century, probably found their limitations on the ancient rivers. Although the later *langskip* or *snekke*, combining wind power with rowing, could go at a speed of more than ten knots, the tidal conditions with a range of eight metres – an unknown factor in the Scandinavian and Baltic areas – and the meandering course of the river with its many banks and low islands did not allow such an effective speed on a waterway penetrating into an unfamiliar hinterland, hiding a military resistance.

For a Viking ship to travel from the estuary to Rouen (c. 120 kilometres) in two days, as the contemporary chronicles tell, seems improbable, as the same journey made by 19th-century boats of comparable tonnage lasted approximately two weeks. This raises the question of the need of pilotage, which remains highly recommended today.

As a consequence the Vikings would have needed a certain experience in navigating the river and its estuary with its capes, behind which they had to await the rising tide (*le flot*) to cross the bars. The first strategic section upstream, between Saint-Wandrille and Jumièges, was accessible by sail, thereafter it was necessary to row. It is obvious that this pivot zone of navigation was a significant landmark on the "mental map" of the Viking seamen, probably materialised in a harbour settlement on the shore. In this connection the mentions in the written sources of the return of the Viking fleets to the river shores at Jumièges for repairing their ships are remarkable.[37]

Moreover, this landmark, achieved through experience, was probably used as a starting point for measuring distances. From Old Norse we know the basic unit *viku*, which is equivalent to the distance covered by an oarsman before being relayed; this measurement was estimated to six sea-miles, which is 11,112 metres.[38] Six *vikur* constituted a rowing day of thirty six sea-miles, which equals 40 kilometres.

To reach "the Winds End" near Jumièges one day of sailing may be needed to cross the estuary and reach the first two meanders, a distance of sixty two kilometres. It takes a day of rowing upstream to reach Rouen, two

Laurent Mazet-Harhoff

days to Les Andelys, and seven days to Paris. Obviously these durations have to be taken with reservations, because they do not take the meanderings of the river and the effects of the current into account, which can either shorten or lengthen the distances covered, or the tide; the high-tide pressure helps to go upstream.

Altogether it can be suggested that the morphology of the lower Seine river in the Viking Age determined the number of sailing and rowing days of the Viking fleets in the three main geographical transport zones of the valley: the estuary, the river from the meanders up to the confluences of the rivers Eure and Andelle, and the section upstream from Poses-Amfreville.

In February when the river is in spate or in August when the water level is low it is difficult to cross some of the meanders. Consequently it may be suggested that some shortcuts across land were used, in particular along the natural corridor which connects Jumièges with Duclair (*c.* 3 km vs. 18 km), or 10 km upstream from Rouen, between Oissel and Criquebeuf-sur-Seine via Tourville-la-Rivière (*c.* 3 km vs. 17 km), in order to avoid the rapids in the meander at Elbeuf. This kind of military operation seems to have been a well known if not significantly usual in the continental context. The Annals of Metz report for 888 that Vikings leaving the river Loing (between Paris and Sens) hauled their ships over nearly two miles, then launched back into the Seine from the bank on which they set up a camp.[39]

The Viking chief Weland may have besieged other Vikings on the island of *Oscellus* on the River Seine in 861 against a ransom from Charles the Bald. After having sailed up the affluent named *Tellas*[40] a part of his fleet pulled its ships across the few kilometres of land to get back on the Seine and may have taken back the famished Viking bastion, which may have given Weland all its treasures.[41] Afterwards the losers may have joined him and according to their respective position they may have established themselves in every port of the Seine from there to Paris. This confusing episode is actually at the heart of the controversy about the localisation of the insular bastion.[42] If, as it has been suggested by Walther Vogel,[43] *Oscellus* is the Grande Ile between Bonnières-sur-Seine and Jeufosse, the river *Tellas* affluent may be the river Epte, which joins the Seine downstream. It does not seem probable, however, that a significant fleet passed the isthmus that exists between Gasny and La Vacherie on the Seine upstream from Bonnières; the land to be crossed has a rise that exceeds eighty metres. On the other hand, if *Oscellus* is indeed close to Oissel, this position might justify Charles the Bald's readiness to pay Weland to overpower the attackers downstream his palace at Pîtres. There was, in any case, no affluent in the area allowing such hauling operation. However, it does not exclude an operation in two stages: a fleet, already based on the river Andelle in order to negotiate with Charles the Bald at *Pistis*, could have sailed down the Seine and across the meander via Tourville-la-Rivière.

As it is regularly mentioned in the written sources, the confluence zone between Pont-de-l'Arche and Pîtres was a very important strategic area both for the Frankish defence – Charles the Bald started the construction of a strengthened bridge there in 862 – and for the Viking fleets, which met there several times thanks to constant accessibility and to many surrounding "land-marks", such as Côte des Deux Amants which dominated the confluent of the river Andelle, a natural headland impossible to miss or to forget for forthcoming raids. Further upstream from Poses the only strategic obstructions were probably the river fords, towards which the ancient roads led, such as near Les Andelys and at the confluence with the river Epte downstream where a ford was formed by the Grande Ile between Bennecourt and Bonnières.

Actually, sailing the only 150 kilometres, which separate the estuary from the confluences of the Rivers Eure and Andelle, needed more time for awaiting good sailing conditions than time for actual sailing, but the effect of the tide, which reached this zone, made it possible to get through all year round. At this point it is relevant to notice that the concentration of place-names of Scandinavian origin in Upper Normandy is concentrated at this particular section of the Seine.

The role of the Seine's affluents must not be underestimated, since some of them, still navigable at that time, were also very useful ways to penetrate into the hinterland: on the right bank we have the river Austreberthe, which joins the Seine at Duclair, and the Eure, which together with the Risle form the main axes cutting the southern bank of the Seine. The river Risle has, however, a slight advantage, as its confluence offers a first shelter to ships crossing the estuary at strong tides.

If the Vikings had not made use of a favourable tide on this river stretch, their hazardous advance would have been slowed down, and had thus required several stop-overs. To travel by boat remained the fastest solution. The ancient roman roads, which connected Harfleur and Rouen pass-

Laurent Mazet-Harhoff

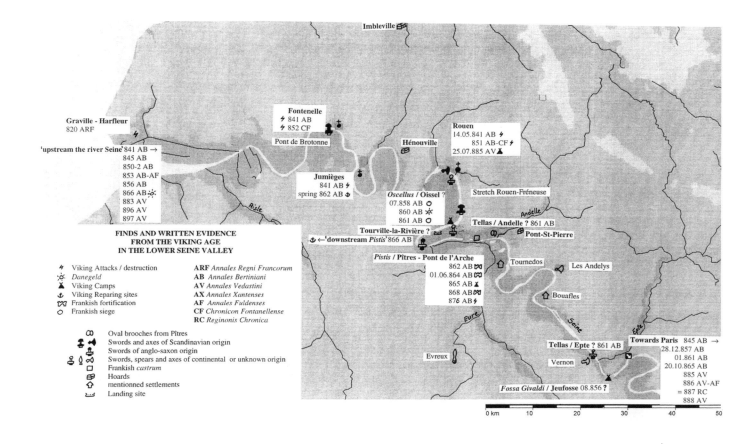

Fig. 2. Finds and written evidence from the Viking Age in the lower Seine valley.

ing steep hills and small valleys, were less efficient in terms of time, energy and logistics.

On the other hand, the river section upstream from Poses was twice as long along its northern bank and followed a level road connecting the fords towards Paris. It is probable that armies on ships were led by this section of the Seine, but that the surprise attacks on Paris in 861 were supported by mounted forces, such as it is mentioned in the *Vita et Miraculi Sancti Germani*.[44]

The incursion of the Vikings into the natural and cultural landscape

The settlement phase: Scandinavian presence in the cultural landscape of Upper Normandy

Among the early isolated finds labelled "Viking"[45] and without a stratigraphic context are fourteen fragments of weapons found during dredging works on the Seine near places mentioned in Carolingian texts (see fig. 2). Among them were only two long swords with semicircular pommel, found at the bridge of Brotonne close to Saint-Wandrille and between Elbeuf and Rouen (1882–1884), which belong to the Scandinavian Petersen's type *Bredvold* W, dated to AD 900–1000.[46] Also Scandinavian are the two battle-axes found in the area of Rouen, one with symmetrical edge and symmetrical hafting lobes (Petersen's type G) dated to AD 850–900, the other with asymmetrical edge (Petersen's type M) dated to AD 875–925.

In addition there are six other swords, three battle-axes and one spearhead of Scandinavian types found between Oissel and Fréneuse, and at Les Andelys and Vernon, which illustrate a possible confusion of indigenous Carolingian artefacts: Petersen's sword types P, *Torshov* H and Jakobsson's type B, dated successively between 700 and 825 on the continent, and on the other hand weapons (some of them Anglo-Saxon) inspired by continental features and spread over Northern Europe: Petersen's types *Skaaden* Y, *Ovri* M and *Hagerbakken* X, dated between AD 850 and 1000.

In spite of their small number, the geographical distribution of these weapons is not random. The find locations correspond to places quoted in the Carolingian chronicles. Even if these finds easily could be interpreted as evidences of battles, in particular on the section Oissel-Pont-de-l'Arche, where the Scandinavian and Frankish forces met, their very fragmentary state rather suggests that they were discarded in the river as broken or worn-down weapons. Therefore, it is necessary only to regard these finds as evidence of Vikings passing these stretches.

At the moment only metallographic analysis would be able to distinguish continental Carolingian products from artefacts of Scandinavian origin. And only few of these weapons have been sufficiently examined. Moreover, the relative abundance of these river finds in Western Europe suggests a possible votive function. Apart from the accidental loss, or the discarded weapon after battle, there are only a few examples described and located to these rivers by contemporary sources. However, thanks to a synoptic re-examination of these finds in progress, we may bring new results in that field.

Laurent Mazet-Harhoff

Among the evidence for the advance of the Vikings into Francia are the Carolingian hoards. Out of the 78 treasures deposited between 798 and 898,[47] 38 are coin hoards dated between 840 and 870. Although civil wars and raids occurred in this period, local insecurity and repeated attacks might not be direct evidence for these hoards' position; the loss of these treasures may also testify to the disappearance of their local owners, killed or detained as slaves or simply escaped to a safer place, a fortified city as Rouen for instance.

The number of hoards dated to this period in Upper Normandy is limited to three depositions, and, significantly, none of these contained Scandinavian or British coins. At Hénouville north-west of Rouen sixty Carolingian coins minted under the rule of Louis the Pious between 822 and 840 were found in 1996. This relatively homogeneous hoard suggests that coins gathered during eighteen years may have been hidden by a resident from this part of the Seine valley that had been devastated after 840.

The hoard of Imbleville, discovered in 1840 in the heart of the Pays de Caux in the Saâne river valley, contained sixty-six silver coins from the reign of Charles the Bald,[48] and comprises a very broad range of coins minted between 864 and 877 in northern Francia: Rouen (eighteen coins), Quentovic, Amiens, Saint-Denis, but also Reims, Soissons, Senlis and Tours. Even if the deposition of this hoard is not easily datable, it follows a tradition of coin hoarding with which the Vikings were familiar.

Finally, the hoard from Pont-Saint-Pierre, north-east of the confluence of the rivers Eure and Andelle, consisted of coins dated to the period 869–877, and was found in an area that saw many conflicts between the Vikings and the Frankish army.

The hoards found along the River Seine confirm the importance of the river valley as a main route of incursion. These hoards are, however, exceptions, as very few hoards from the same period (822–877) have been found north of the Seine, an area that was significantly disturbed by the Vikings. On the other hand, several examples of hoards, dated to the end of the reign of Charles the Bald and the beginning of that of Louis the Pious' towards 900, have been found in small concentrations north-west of the Seine and between the Seine and the river Loire. These hoards appear at the theatre of operation of the "Great Army" (879–884), whose camp was located probably at Choisy-au-Bac (on the river Oise, affluent of the Seine), near Ablaincourt and Glisy (Somme).

The incursion of the Vikings into the natural and cultural landscape

Among these isolated finds we have to mention not least the famous oval brooches from Pîtres, found in a female grave in 1865, and which therefore were not subject to any stratigraphic analysis. This pair of tortoise-shaped brooches in gilt bronze may be related to Petersen's type 40 (Rygh 657), which occurred in Scandinavia, and in Norway in particular, between AD 850 and 900.[49]

The burial from Pîtres is central to the debate of the scale of the Viking colonisation in Normandy, and for the discussion of the extent of cultural assimilation of the Scandinavians into the local population. The assumption that any Scandinavian tradition (and thus any Scandinavian features in the material culture) quickly disappeared, owing to marriages between members of the exclusively male crews and female members of the population of Neustria, stands in contrast to information given by some of the written sources.

Thanks to Abbo of Rheims's account on the Siege of Paris[50] we know that women followed their men on the raids and they encouraged them to fight; they took care of the food supplies. Furthermore, Scandinavia could be reached in less than a week by boat and thus nothing could prevent the Vikings from bringing back women and children and to settle permanently. From another source it is known that under the founders of the Norman Duchy, polygamy was institutionalised under the name of "marriage *a more danico*", which does not exclude the possibility of mixed marriage where Scandinavian and Frankish wives coexisted.

More specific, a parallel can be drawn to Britain, where the Scandinavian presence was not limited to seasonal raids. Indeed, Viking warriors might have settled with their partners quite far inland.[51] If the male burials found there were characterised by Anglo-Saxon or Carolingian weapons, the female burials, rich in the usual furnishing, display a significant homogeneity compared to the Scandinavian contexts. Altogether, the British burials, as a parallel to the Norman context, illustrate a very clear decline in the tradition of cremation compared to Scandinavia, and an increasing number of burials in mounds, which primary function could have been a deliberate territorial marking of significant militarily zones, near the Danelaw border in particular.[52]

In comparison with the funerary customs practised by the Vikings in the British Isles, one notices the similar location of the grave at Pîtres, namely, near a pre-existing cultural place, the Gallo-Roman crypt at Pierre-

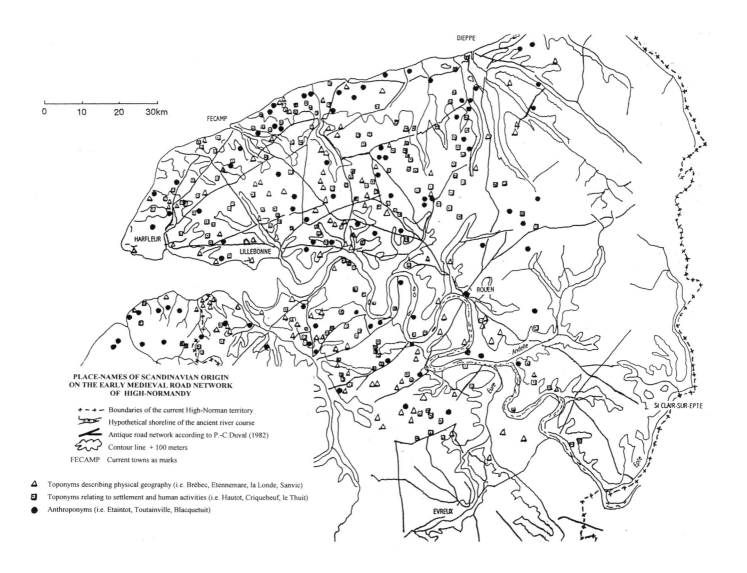

Fig. 3. Place-names of Scandinavian origin on the Early Medieval road network of Upper Normandy.

Saint-Martin, excavated by Leon Coutil in 1899, where there was no evidence of contemporaneity with the Viking burial.[53]

From Scandinavia it is known that the Vikings also went on horse or by foot, and were able to open or follow tracks through the forests, avoiding marshes and peat bogs, and to cross fords or isthmuses with their ships, which they hauled by hand or with horses. Hill tops, natural obstacles, and traces of hu-

The incursion of the Vikings into the natural and cultural landscape

man activities in the maritime landscape were the landmarks of their mental map. Commercial contacts with the many coastal markets in the Baltic and the North Sea areas were easily linkable within a few days by boat, and at the same time conveyed much information about treasures and territories to be conquered, about roads to follow, and about obstacles to avoid.

This cognitive context leads us to create a corpus of the remains of the Vikings in Upper Normandy, among which the most discussed evidence are the toponyms and micro-toponyms of Scandinavian origin (see fig. 3).[54]

The heavy concentration of these place-names suggests a dense Scandinavian occupation in the present territory of Upper Normandy. However, it is important to remember that this cartographic picture is the cumulative result of a process that probably started in the Viking Age, of colonisation and cognitive control of a territory, but to which it is necessary to add later similar toponyms, because of dialectal impregnation caused by foreign imports.

In order to go into detail with the toponymic chronology, we have tried to superimpose the map of the toponyms of Scandinavian origin onto the map of the ancient river-systems with their network of Roman roads,[55] of which many sections through the unpopulated and densely wooded Pays de Caux were still used in the Early Middle Ages, by the Frankish armies in particular.[56] By highlighting the 100 metre level of the contour map it was possible to identify the hill tops as potential landmarks along the coasts and river banks.

On basis of their etymological meaning,[57] I have chosen three main types of toponyms: 1) toponyms describing physical geography such as Roumare (of Norse *marr*, "the pond"), Bolbec (*bekkr*, "the brook"), Ficquefleur (*flodr*, "the river, the fjord"), La Londe (*lundr*, "the wood, the thicket"), Sanvic ("the sandy split"), and Dieppedale ("the deep valley"); 2) those related to human activities and settlement such as the multiple place-names with the endings -tot (*toft*, "the ground to build"), -beuf (*both*, "the hangar, the hut"), and -thuit (*Þveit*, "the essart, the clearance"), and finally 3) the anthroponyms combining personal names with the suffix -ville, as in Barneville, Vatteville, Amfreville.

It is remarkable that most of the place-names related to natural sites are placed at valley slopes and on the road network. The anthroponyms combining personal names with the suffix -ville, pointing out settlements from Late Antiquity and the Merovingian period, more often occupy crossroad zones and river fords. Finally, the toponyms relating to the Scandinavian agrarian unit *toft* ("the inhabited ground, the croft"), which developed to -tot, are spread further inland along marginal routes which form today's local and regional public thoroughfares. In other words, these toponyms relating to settlement seem to mark the step from the ancient interregional road system towards the more local road system of the Medieval Period, still maintained in modern times and gradually fixed since the 19th century.

Compared to the land- and waterways, the distribution of the toponyms raises three questions: Was the network of nature-related landmarks established during an early identification of the roads by the Vikings? May anthroponyms given to existing crossroad sites prove the use of strategic landmarks at the road system? For toponyms relating to settlements, dispersed along marginal routes, may they indicate a later establishment of Scandinavian settlements outside already populated or colonised areas, like at the Pays de Caux or the periphery of Rouen?

Obviously, these issues, reinforced by the incapacity of the linguists to date the exact appearance of these place names, lead to an essential question in our research, which we, however, cannot solve here: to measure the demographic and cultural impact of the "colonists" compared to the indigenous population. This means either to identify the factors that made it possible for a minority of occupants to control an area, or to examine the integration of newcomers, regularly arriving and increasing the settlements of the new lands. These tempting assumptions are not easily provable on a regional scale and, therefore, it seems more preferable to study the situation on a smaller scale, by relating toponyms and micro-toponyms to the local archaeological survey.

The Seine valley would deserve to be examined on a micro-toponymic scale. These place names lead to many considerations such as Les Malmains for example (GPS 5476.5 N; 346 E), which identify the digging sites for the so-called ferruginous *Malm* in a Scandinavian context in the Viking Age. This micro-toponym of the meander of Jumièges faces Conihout-sous-Jumièges (GPS 5474.5 N; 342 E), where excavations at the coast recorded by Abbé Cochet in the 19th century recovered pits of unspecified origin that the inhabitants called Les Trous fumeux or Les Trous de fer, "the smoky holes" or "iron holes".[58] Should this type of evidence with logistic connotation pointing out iron reducing kilns and forging activities not be taken into account when, according to the Annals of St Bertin for 862 and later Dudo of Saint-Quentin, the Vikings established their hibernal shipyard in this zone?

Some other remarkable Frankish assimilated micro-toponyms might sustain St Bertin's and Dudo's quotations about a maritime / fluvial base there, as "le Druglan" (GPS 5477.75 N; 341.5 E) from the Old Norse *drjúg* "draw out over a long shore" (*land*), which may signal a permanent landing place in-between the monastic foundation at Jumièges and the actual river bank. On the opposite bank, "la Vette" (GPS 5479 N, 340.5 E), which appears as a Frankish form of the Old Norse *Vetr* "winter", might be connected to a hibernal shelter for the tidal phenomenon and simultaneously at a secure but controlling distance from one of the main strategic economical centres in the lower Seine valley at that time.

As for the meeting places for fleets, there are also some common traits to the micro-toponymic evidence mentioned in the written evidence. Whereas the supposed island of Jeufosse, referring to the archipelago of the meander of Bonnières, should be understood as the Grande Ile and the Ile de la Flotte, the area near Pîtres also counts a Grande Ile as well as a landing place named Les Flotteaux (GPS 2480.5 N; 520 E), which one would be tempted to bring closer to the Danish toponym *Flådeå* pronounced [floðœ-o], which means from the Old Norse *floti* and *à* "the river of the fleet".

After these somewhat superficial and speculative observations on the relevance of the regional distribution of toponyms compared to the transport and communication network, it is obvious that this evidence on its own could not identify Scandinavian settlements in Upper Normandy. However, the toponymic connection to the former environment and the archaeological map, known on a local scale, would deserve to be taken into account. In the Seine valley in particular, micro-toponyms of Scandinavian maritime origin are still unexamined, which suggest an archaeological potential, related to the early and durable presence of the invaders in the lower Seine area, a no man's land which became a *base-arrière* for Viking incursions.

Fortified places: Witnesses of colonisation?

Fortified places are among structures which might testify to the Viking progression into the Frankish territory, but were the Vikings confronted

Laurent Mazet-Harhoff

with Frankish fortifications when they arrived? Did the Vikings themselves have to build fortresses to support their advance or did they simply reuse pre-existing fortifications? In other words, do the many mounds and other Norman moated sites from 10th and 11th centuries go back to the Scandinavian invasion?

In the archaeological record of Upper Normandy two distinct, rather well-documented, chronological phases can be identified: the so-called proto-historic retrenchments and the medieval moated sites.

The existence of more than twenty fortified places from the La Téne period following the large river valleys draws the attention to the strategic character of the river a thousand years before the Scandinavian invasions.[59] And one may wonder whether these barred promontories with simple or multiple ramparts, dominating the valley, could be reused for protection by the local population or even by the Vikings during their attacks. These enclosures of several tens of hectares, suitable for sheltering of a significant work force, occupy the unavoidable peaks in the valley near the confluences or among the outer cliffs of the meanders. However, many have argued that these sites could not even protect the local Gallo-Roman population against the Saxons, and no reoccupation has been detected until the 3rd century AD. Moreover, reforestation, which covered antique sites of the area already in the Merovingian Period, melted these "panoramic platforms" into the general landscape. If the Vikings had used them for temporary observation posts, the access from the bottom of the valley was so difficult that a Viking army could settle there for long and could ensure the protection of its fleet.

Another fortification, by the written sources related directly to the Scandinavian presence in the valley, is the famous bridge at *Pistis*, fortified on the command of Charles the Bald in 862. Localisation of the structures downstream the confluence of the Eure and the Seine between Pont-de-l'Arche on the left bank and Igoville is based partly on the archaeological excavations carried out on the right bank by Brian Dearden (University of Manchester).[60]

According to Dearden, the strengthened bridge was actually a fortification of the heads of a pre-existing bridge at this place providing the passage of an ancient road. If archaeological documentation ensures neither the ancient bridge nor a simultaneous fortification on the left bank, the discovery of a rampart with a palisade strengthened by an external ditch on the right bank, however, attests to the construction of a quadrangular enclosure, approximately 250 by 250 metres. Repeated improvements of the constructions using a combination of masonry and wooden frames seem to have prevented the *castrum* from destruction by fire or by a rising water level in the river. Indeed, already in its first phase, the structure had been prepared for such risky situations by using argillaceous fill, which remained resistant to the river variations.

The relationship between this site and the events which, according to the written sources, occurred on the Seine between 862 and 886, the supposed date of the destruction of the bridge is to be taken with a pinch of salt. The dating evidence is indeed very weak; only a preserved fragment of a wooden frame used for the reinforcement of the rampart, was C14-dated to AD 860 +/- 40. In addition, the very restricted excavation could not clarify the internal occupation of the enclosure.

Among the existing sites from the invasions along the lower Seine, mentioned by the written sources or, more rarely, archaeologically identified, only two sites proved to be earlier than the 10th century[61] and they seem to be characterised by their proximity to the river and by their topographic position[62] – the site called Radicatel at the lower Seine close to Lillebonne and probably the promontory retrenchment at Le Catelier on the Plateau des Aigles at Bonsecours, dominating Rouen.[63] In Jacques Le Maho's opinion these defensive sites, which are mentioned in the written sources of the 8th century and were constructed on promontories, at Radicatel in the shape of a terrace and in the case of Bonsecours a barricade, were built under the first Carolingian earls of Neustria. Many mentions in the written sources and much toponymic evidence refer to on the one hand their defeat during the first Viking attacks and, on the other, to their reoccupation by the ducal power in the 10th century. The intermediate sequence, however, does not manifest itself in the Carolingian written sources, nor in the field.

From 855–856 and onwards, after only about fifteen years of continuous incursions into the Lower Seine area, retrenchments were built by the Vikings, as mentioned in the Carolingian Annals and Chronicles. The need for stopovers and camps emerged as the Vikings understood that the areas immediately around the river did not offer any more treasures, whereas operations of a greater scale into the hinterland could be profitable. Because of the

Laurent Mazet-Harhoff

use of cavalry in their army they needed meeting places that could function as bases for future raids as well. They needed retreats, warehouses for the spoils and probably enclosures for the hostages, enrolled or submitted to slavery.[64]

In the descriptions of the camps built by the Vikings in the lower Seine valley given in the Carolingian and ducal written sources three types of retrenchments appear:

a) The natural retrenchments like the Morin Island in Rouen. *Oscellus* and Jeufosse were doubtless left in their primitive state. However, in the sections under tidal influence, constructed quays or banks could be necessary. Furthermore, the Vikings had to build dwellings using local materials.

Of the stopovers on the islands mentioned in the written sources none have been subject to any investigation. However, in the archaeological inventory of Les Haugues south of Jumièges from 1835 the remains of an enclosure surrounded by a ditch in the middle of the marshes of Conihout-sous-Jumièges are recorded.[65]

For the stretch between Harfleur and Rouen it is possible that some low islands, which have now disappeared or been connected with the mainland, sheltered very temporary stopovers during the first summer raids, when the neap tides reduced the water level of the river. On the other hand, when at equinox the water level was rising and the *mascaret* occurred the Vikings certainly preferred the permanent shelter of their usual targets for stopovers: the abbeys of the valley.

b) Monastic enclosures as Saint-Wandrille/Fontenelle and Jumièges probably sheltered raiders for a rather long period. For example, the Miracles of Saint Bertin reports for 2 May 891 state that the occupants of the abbey built "huts of planks and straw [...] as they use to do it for a long stay"[66] in the gardens. However, one may doubt the strategic value of a base within the very walls of the abbeys where the Vikings themselves were likely to be besieged by the Frankish defence. The Viking bases were more likely placed at a calculated distance from those local administrative centres that the Frankish power had good reasons to defend. To date no archaeological excavation at the monastic sites of the lower Seine has identified temporary occupations *intra muros* or *in claustra*.

The incursion of the Vikings into the natural and cultural landscape

c) For the ring-shaped fortifications erected *ex nihilo* by the Vikings there are several designations in the Frankish texts. They describe either a circular rampart adapted to the size of the involved army, or a half-circular retrenchment which bars a naturally defended site on one or several sides.

In an analysis of Dudo of Saint Quentin's work on the period covering Hastings, Rollo's activities and the reigns of William Longsword and Richard I, a range of terms distinguishing small temporary fortifications in rural or half-rural areas (*munimen, munitio, munitissima loca, castellum*) from more usual urban or surrounding fortifications (*urbs, civitas, moenia, oppidum, castrum*) have been recorded.[67] Dudo describes in particular a *munimen* as the camp established by Rollo close to Pont-de-l'Arche, and of which the trenched structures were still visible in his time: "Meanwhile Rollo and those who were with him have made for themselves a fortification, and an obstacle after the fashion of a fortress, defending themselves behind a circular bulwark of rent earth, and leaving ample space to act as a gate".[68]

William of Jumièges reports also that "Rollo and those who were with him, erected some retrenchments and a defence in the shape of a *castellum*, strengthening them-selves behind a bank of earth and leaving as a gate, a large opened space".[69]

In Duisburg on the Rhine, the use of earth strengthened with stones[70] is reported as "the accustomed manner"[71] to raise these fortifications doubled with a ditch and sometimes provided with a palisade. In this source it is mentioned that in 886, to establish their camp close to the church of Saint-Germain l'Auxerrois, "they encircled it with some ditches, they were one foot wide and three feet deep, only cut by some paths, necessary for comings and goings".

This hierarchy of camps seems to depend on their different military use and on their accessibility from the rivers or the inland. In difference to simple transitory stages in a recognising and offensive approach, a retreat requires secure and strategic sites, probably selected among the precedent stopovers. In addition, even if these camps may be naturally or artificially well defended, they have to be easily accessible, in particular from the waterway, but also from the road which, the other way round, guarantees an optimum range for such a camp.

On a logistic plan, naturally defended sites seem to meet the strategic needs of a limited armed force, while a fortification raised *ex nihilo* might testify to a much more significant force, not only having sufficient manpower for heavy work, but also the capacity of defending the site under construction. That said, it also has to be admitted that the size of the established camps decreases with the progression farther inland.

The few descriptions of Viking camps, although very vague on the details of their fortification structures or topography, provide invaluable information for a comparison with the archaeological evidence of similar sites in other contexts. This applies in particular to peninsular sites, comprising a D-shaped fortification supplementing the natural defences on one or more sides (coast, confluence, marsh, and headland).

Indeed, one cannot omit the wall-and-ditch fortifications from Britain that are connected to Scandinavian incursions through several mentions in the Anglo-Saxon Chronicle during the years 865–870. In addition to the D-shaped camp in Repton, which by a multiple burial is dated to the years 873–874, many other D-shaped sites are still controversial such as Church Spanel (Shillington, Bedfordshire), Stonea Camp (Wimblington, Bedfordshire), and Shoebury (Essex), which present varied combinations of walls doubled with ditches. These sites, found along the border of the Danelaw, are steadily reduced in size the further one goes inland. The coastal camp at Shoebury mentioned in 893 with a diameter of 460 metres may shelter the men of a massive fleet. Located more than 100 km inland the camp at Repton displays more modest dimensions (approximately 150 metres in diameter) without being less demanding from a logistic point of view: it has been estimated that it took approximately two hundred men five weeks to build its two hundred metres long entrenchment.[72]

Altogether, the archaeological potential of the lower Seine regarding fortified sites met or established by the Vikings still remains to be evaluated as the investigations of the Frankish and ducal periods are so far still too sporadic.

The impact of the Vikings on the rural settlement

In contrast to the brutality of the Viking attacks in Neustria, described in the many Carolingian mentions, their impact ought to be very slight, considering the small number of contemporaneous settlements, that have been excavated in the area. However, traces of Viking occupation can be sought

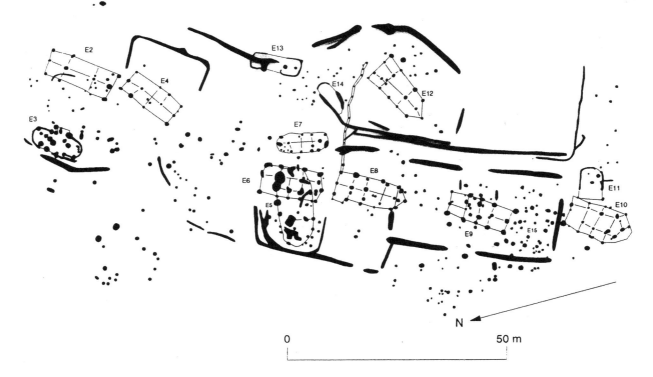

Fig. 4. The Medieval settlement at Bouafles, "Les Mousseaux". Plan over the medieval structures and main hypothesis for restitution of the dwellings. Notice the location of the curvilinear house E5. C. Billard and P. Fournier 1996.

with two opposite scenarios in mind: on the one hand, a direct identification of "imported" artefact shapes and building customs, known in the Vikings' homelands and expansion area, and on the other hand, traces of an indirect impact on the general settlement organisation.

In Bouafles/Les Mousseaux (see fig. 4), on the right bank of the Seine between Gaillon and Les Andelys, we have noticed an anomaly, interesting for our research, during the rescue excavation led by Cyril Billard and Pascal Fournier.[73] Apart from a circular house dated to the Late Bronze Age the settlement presents a range of thirteen dwellings of bow-sided or rectangular plan and with or without an apse. An extremely homogeneous but unevenly distributed material dated to the 11th–12th centuries was found at the site. One of the bow-sided houses, the oldest house according to the stratigraphy, is characterised not only by its division into three aisles, but also by its East-West orientation, which contrasts with the orientation of the banks of the River Seine, which runs from south to north. Later buildings are, however, aligned parallel with the river banks.

Without drawing any hasty conclusion, the features of this house – E5 on the plan – recalls the bow-sided houses with three aisles known primarily from western Denmark during the 8th and 9th centuries.[74]

The settlement site at Tournedos-sur-Seine / Val-de-Reuil (Eure) (see fig. 5) provides the single regional example of settlement continuity through the entire Medieval Period (7th–14th centuries).[75] Already occupied since the Neolithic period, the site of Portejoie – about 500 metres from the River

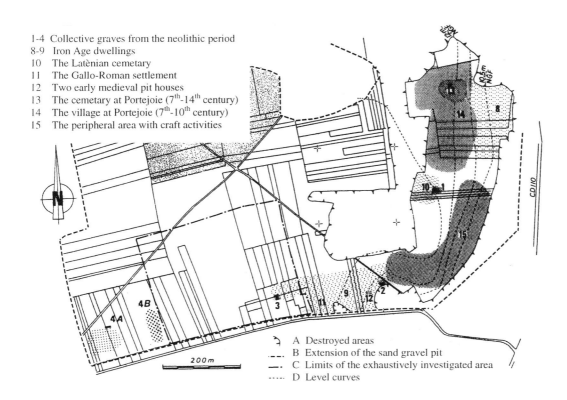

Fig. 5. The Early Medieval settlement at Tournedos-sur-Seine / Val-de-Reuil. Distribution of the settlement areas compared to the local cadaster and topographic curves. Fl. Carré, February 1993.

The incursion of the Vikings into the natural and cultural landscape

Seine, upstream and south-east of the confluence of the River Eure – covers six hectares on which a village was revealed by its hollow structures, a cemetery and a peripheral zone of activity, also rich in trenched structures.

The chronological analysis of the site was seriously limited by the quasi-lack of soil layers and structures allowing relative dating. Primarily based on thin ceramic evidence, the settlement around the cemetery was in continuous use during the 7th–10th centuries, later marked by the church Sainte-Cécile, which in mentions of 1006 and 1025 is associated with the status of *Portus Gaudii*.

The settlement apparently consist of 72 *Grubenhäuser* of 10 to 15 square metres each. Moreover, no domestic furnaces were recorded and no grain silos either, although they are common in other contemporary sites. Thanks to an examination of the grave goods comprising some metal objects, however in most cases only ceramics, it was possible to connect the cemetery with the settlement. In some plots East-West oriented fences and groups of structures each with their own well, warehouses, pits, and 7–11 probably inhabited huts were gathered around a dwelling whose only remaining trace is the regular surface inbetween. The settlement seems to move during the 10th century, but the cemetery was still in use thereafter.

A vast number of *Grubenhäuser*, pits, six wells of which one contains a dated plank, and nine houses of square or rectangular plan with four to six posts appeared south of the village during the 9th–10th centuries. Close to these buildings a number of pits were recorded, some with homogeneous fill and others containing green cobnuts, remains of furnaces with traces of wattle, slag or agrarian tools (ploughshare, forgings, and sickles). The contemporary burials in the cemetery do not comprise any furnishing. Therefore, chronology is based on a typology of the grave pits, and the horizontal stratigraphy of the cemetery. The move of the settlement during the 10th century allowed an extension of the cemetery in this sector. The details of the anthropological studies of the skeletal material from the 9th- and 10th-century graves are, however, not accessible yet, and the grave goods found in the peripheral zone are still under study.

Those characteristics of the settlement at Tournedos that are related to the Scandinavian presence in the area comprise a number of small details, judged on the basis of the accessible documentation.

A significant zone of homogeneous economic activity, which emerges in the periphery of the existing village during the 9th and 10th centuries,

Laurent Mazet-Harhoff

claims attention, especially because this new settlement phase is associated with a change in funerary custom – an increase in individual burials with no coffins and with disappearance of grave goods – and involves a displacement of the pre-existing village. Unless current investigations show foreign anthropological traits of the skeletons, the continuous use of the cemetery suggests, in spite of a change in burial custom, a continuance of the population *in situ*, who was forced to give up its traditional burial practice because of a rapidly increasing number of dead (only 68 burials from 7th–8th centuries whereas more than 1600 burials from the whole settlement period). The population was probably forced to preserve or to re-use the objects they used as grave goods before.

In addition, the peripheral zone comprises, apart from remains of burnt corn, no indications of the presence of a silo, which would have proved agrarian activities. And the presence of a combination of some pits with homogeneous filling and others with filling of rubbish recalls the pattern of some contemporary Scandinavian markets, such as the coastal site of Sebbersund in the eastern Limfjord, northern Jutland,[76] which was also organised in three specialised zones, or the landing-place at Skuldevig/Lynæs in the northern Roskilde Fjord, where shallow pits lined with clay revealed the existence of tent grounds for seasonal settlements.[77]

The phase of integration: The Viking impact on regional developments

Whereas our knowledge of the urban development in the entire lower Seine valley has many lacunae, because of insufficient archaeological investigations in the secondary ports of the valley, the urban excavations in Rouen stand as a privileged source of information because of the city's singular ambiance in the Viking Age: it was the first continental Episcopal target of the Scandinavian raids and paradoxically it became the capital of the only Scandinavian colony which was maintained in the Frankish kingdom.

On the eve of the Scandinavian incursions, Rouen offered an urban landscape which was largely inherited from the Late Antiquity (see fig. 6). The Gallo-Roman walls and roadway system still existed as did also the road infrastructure connecting the city with its rural periphery on which its economy depended. At the beginning of the 9th century, the city harboured the main seats of both the laic and the ecclesiastical authorities, among

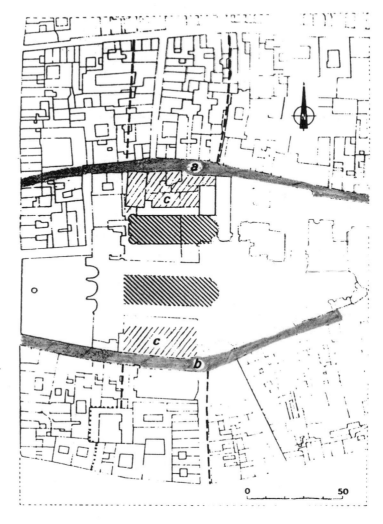

Fig. 6. The urban development of Rouen in the 10th century. Plan over the bishopric group and annexes of Rouen around AD 950. a) rue St Romain and b) rue du Change cutting the ancient gallo-roman axes (broken lines). c) the excavated settlement areas. J. Le Maho 1994a.

them monasteries and aristocratic manors. This closed unit was encircled by a suburban cemetery, churches, orchards and a commercial district.

After the first Viking attack in May 841 the burned-down cathedral and monasteries were partly abandoned. The most valuable relics were evacuated, and just as the Episcopal palace was built against the rampart as a tiny fortified room, the city was transformed into a fortified camp. Until 885 the population, which was temporarily protected by the regular payment of *Danegeld*, remained in the city and organised themselves. The suburban cemeteries were abandoned and the relics were transferred *intra-muros*.

From 885, the increasing and more intense Norman attacks forced the Frankish authorities into exile, however, without losing their territorial and administrative power until the beginning of the 10th century. At the same time, economic activity and population from the ports and monastic boroughs of the lower valley escaped towards the city, and thus maintained its dominating Frankish identity, as it can be read in the written sources from the years 940–950.

During the first half of the 10th century significant changes in the urban landscape can be identified. Old properties, inheritances of abbeys and aristocratic families were redistributed to the refugees from the lower valley, who then became new citizens of the city. This repopulation was followed by a reform of the cadastre, whose orientation now became perpendicular to the ancient roadway system inherited from Antiquity. Indeed, along the new East-West axes excavations revealed buildings which were laid out with the house ends facing the street, and dated by ceramics and two coins minted during Louis IV's Overseas' rule to the second half of the 10th century.[78] In rue St Romain a stone building with partitions and a lean-to building with latrines and connected pits were found, and in half-timbered houses with wattle and daub found in rue du Change many building phases were identified together with connected pits which cut the preceding, but now unused, public roads.

If the economic and demographic prosperity of Rouen inside its ramparts seems well-documented after 950, it is, however, still hazardous to link the new urban face of the city to a direct initiative of the Scandinavians, the first of them Rollo. The possibility of an economic renewal of the city even before the Normans (Vikings) took possession of it as a capital has to be considered, especially on the background of the relationship with the other economic actors in the lower valley: namely the monastic centres.

Between 918 and 1026, starting with the foundation of the duchy of Normandy at St Clair-sur-Epte and its political stabilisation under the reign of Richard II, conspicuous economic progress of the new principality took place. Many international exchanges are reflected in the large variety of the coins in the hoard from Fécamp hidden around 980–985.[79] From the same

The incursion of the Vikings into the natural and cultural landscape

period many ports[80] shelled along the coasts and in particular along the Seine emerge in the written sources and testify to a commercial dynamism on a regional and even local level, which precedes a more continental traffic in the middle of the 11th century.[81] The eight ports known on the Seine in Late Antiquity developed into the 27 markets and transit places mentioned during the 12th century.[82] As it is probable that they did not all appear simultaneously in the 12th century, which one of these may then testify to ruptures or to continuous use after the passage of the Scandinavians?

The Viking incursions may have had an impact on the economic development already in progress in the lower Seine valley. The most relevant sites in this respect are the monastic *porti,* which emerged in the 7th century, such as *Logium* / Caudebec, Saint-Wandrille and Jumièges, for which Jacques Le Maho has showed the economic superiority in competition with Rouen before the Vikings arrived.[83] Some of these monastic centres had many harbour concessions along the river. Contrary to the rural settlements of the valley, which preserved their old names and most probably their population and estate system from the 8th to the 11th century, almost every *vici* harbour was renamed with Scandinavian toponyms at the beginning of the 10th century, for example, *Rislecliff* became Quillebeuf / *kjolr-boð*, *Logium* became Caudebec / *kaldr-bekkr*. Probably, such a toponymic change was the consequence of an early settlement of a Scandinavian population in areas which, if not depopulated, was at least deserted by its principal economic actors, who had by then taken refuge in the city of Rouen.

In spite of their destruction during the Scandinavian attacks, some of these monastic centres took part in the restoration of the Norman Church by founding new abbeys and reopening *scriptoria* towards the end of the 10th century; and they re-established their vocation as ports while conveying the stone from Caen partly in order to restore their walls.[84] Although to some extent established on ducal authority, the Church may by and large have been alone in charge of the commercial renewal of the international traffic and activities of the river ports. If the commercial activities at Saint-Wandrille do not reappear until in the middle of the 11th century, as it is quoted in the Miracles of Saint Wulfran,[85] the abbey, formerly placed at the bottom of the estuary, remains comparable to many *emporia* of the North Sea.

Even though no real harbour structures have been recorded at Saint-Wandrille yet, we must, however, call attention to the recent excavations carried out by Hervé Barbé and Michel Barret close to the abbey Saint Bertin in Saint-Omer, originally located on the isthmus of the river Aa in the northern province.[86] In the Carolingian layers from the 9th and 10th centuries, fragments of decorated objects and fragments of leather shoes were found, and the river banks were stabilised with wattle, comparable with those from York and Hedeby/Haithabu. Facing such evidence, one wonders whether this type of structure, which is otherwise absent in Upper Normandy, could have been necessary for the cross-Channel commercial activities as mentioned in the Miracles of Saint Edmond,[87] which describes the cargo of the *isnecchia* or *snekke* that put in at St Wandrille: "sixty men, thirty-six animals and sixteen horses loaded with goods". Such traffic probably caused, if not the development of the monastic ports, at least their restoration. Unfortunately no investigations have been carried out on these sites although the soil conditions of the riverine area seem to guarantee good preservation for waterlogged wooden structures.

For the phase of integration it has to be taken into account that local development was already in progress at the arrival of the Vikings, for example among the settlement areas of the middle Seine valley such as Les Andelys, Meulan Les Mureaux, and Pontoise, where the passage of Scandinavian hordes is attested to during the years 885–892.

These old settlements, which moved until they finally were fixed along the river banks at the bottom of the valley, deserve attention, especially as these early Medieval urban centres developed inside D-shaped defensive ditches dug into the river bank.[88] The *Annales Vedastini* mentions around 884 a *castrum* in Pontoise. In Meulan-Les Mureaux the re-use of the ancient quays at the end of the 9th century is identified as a settlement which is also defended by a D-shaped ditch along the river. At the lower Seine the same pattern is reflected in the general shape of the fortifications at Pont-de-l'Arche / *Pistis*, which was visited by the Vikings several times.[89]

Conclusion: The potential of the archaeological finds from the Viking Age in the Lower Seine valley

The Seine valley had become a *no man's land*, which was, however, successfully repopulated at the very end of the 10th century due to the economic activities. Upper Normandy seems to have been the area which best provided the maritime structures that were attractive for the Scandinavians.

The now boggy banks of the Seine, which modern canalisation has sealed behind dams, offer *a priori* good soil conditions for preservation of organic material, which constitutes a substantial part of two categories of structures that are important for the coastal infra-structure and are well-documented in Scandinavia. And which furthermore will be of interest for future prospection of harbour sites in the Seine valley:

1) Riverbank structures to protect near-river settlements against erosion caused by tide and mooring of boats, and which may form a quay above a marshy zone. On the coastal sites from the Late Iron Age (AD 400–1000) in the southern Baltic area, H. Jankuhn recorded five different types of bank revetments:[90] a) wattle work; b) row of piles; c) row of post and planks; d) horizontal boards with anchoring piles; and e) *bauwerk* with horizontal planks connected with sets of intermediate posts.

Such structures are easily built with a limited force of labour and at short notice, which military logistics usually require. Such structures may also help widen the navigable part of a narrow river.

2) Jetties and docks mark the reclaim of new surfaces beyond the shore line, and also allow access for more heavy-draught boats. The construction of jetties and docks is more time-consuming and needs a higher level of logistic organisation. Three main types appear: a) rows of piles and enhanced wooden quays in the harbour at Dorestad (AD 650–900) and Hedeby/Haithabu (length: 60 m; *c.* AD 720–1050); b) stone jetties in Kaupang, Norway (*c.* AD 800–900), where stones were laid on fascines encircled by lines of piles; c) earth or stone jetties held by wooden structures at Ralswieck (Northern Germany) in AD 850–950, where dug out mooring canals formed side jetties, in Dublin dated to AD 820, at Birka in Sweden around AD 930–950, and in Agdenes around AD 1080, where several tens of metres-long jetties have been recorded. The amount of organisation and labour which these structures required, gives an idea of the investment needed for the transformation of simple stopover places into real harbours of different status.

In the near future it is the duty of archaeology systematically to investigate the riverine areas in order to gain more knowledge about the entrenched camps along the rivers, which allowed the Scandinavians to control their most permanent colony. However, waterfront archaeology, as it has been seen with our British and Scandinavian colleagues who have been

Laurent Mazet-Harhoff

busy for more than twenty years, is up against many scientific, financial and legal obstacles.

On the basis of all the criteria for Scandinavian harbour settlements from the Viking Age and the relevant communications in the Seine valley, as well as Carolingian testimonies, it is possible to identify four archaeologically relevant zones which might contain traces of the maritime activities of the Scandinavians, from their first incursions and to the stabilisation of the Norman duchy:

1) The inter-modal section from St Wandrille to Jumièges, a thousand-year-old transit zone between open sea and river types of transport, is not only the first ford of the Seine, but also a gate to the inland roads. Taking advantage of the isolation of the monastic houses from the general population, who probably stayed in the hinterland since the Saxon invasions, the Vikings could establish relatively safe camps halfway between the vast estuary and the city of Rouen.

2) Upstream from Rouen the tidal effect was less and the islands were safe from regular floods. The archipelago of Oissel may have been a strategic zone of defence and control over the road network converging at the city, in particular when Frankish defence could rely temporarily on the strengthened bridge at *Pistis*.

3) The junction zone near Pîtres and Pont-de-l'Arche was probably a key to the raiding campaigns. As a strategic ford between the coastal region and the river valleys, the confluences of the Eure and Andelle sheltered a safe landing place for repeated fleet meetings. This nodal zone of territorial control had to be the object of the set-up of many harbours and defences, in particular after 911 when Rollo was engaged by Charles the Simple to fight (or to divert) new Viking incursions into Norman territory. For this reason one may suppose that the multiple arms of the confluence of the river Eure were controlled or barred by means of piles or scuttled ship-wrecks.

4) Finally, the meander at Jeufosse near Bonnières-sur-Seine, although disputed as the locality of the *Oscellum* Island, is likely to be the right area to investigate. No canalizing operations have been recorded there during the last 1000 years. In other terms, possible archaeological evidence from the

The incursion of the Vikings into the natural and cultural landscape

Viking Age should have remained quite undisturbed on this permanently navigable river strech. Located not far from the confluence of the river Epte, Jeufosse, up to which the Vikings sailed after 850 when they negotiated the eastern border of the duchy, forms a Norman outpost, at a strategic stage between Rouen and Paris.

To conclude: This paper, which is mainly one long scheme of intentions for future research, discusses the complexity of the Viking question. In an area where the density of toponyms of Scandinavian origin suggests a wide range of related and identifiable remains, we saw, however, that the types of sources to be analysed and the processes going on at that time were numerous, just as was the case in Scandinavia at the same time: a territorial unification under a sovereign, a commercial progress supporting the urban development, and the progress of the Church following Christianisation. It would be quite simplistic, however, to believe that these changes, which characterised north-western Europe around AD 1000, were the legacy of the Vikings alone.

Laurent Mazet-Harhoff

Notes

1 Lair 1897: 2–39.
2 Lot 1970.
3 Musset 1965.
4 D'Haenens 1970: 95–106.
5 Fellows-Jensen 1994a & 1994b.
6 Chatellier & Le Pontois 1908.
7 Müller-Wille 1978.
8 Elmqvist 1969.
9 Price 1989.
10 Périn 1990.
11 Le Maho 1994a & 1994b.
12 Mazet 1996: 11–32.
13 Ulriksen 1997: 182–195.
14 Mcgrail 1985.
15 Westerdahl 1992: 5–14.
16 Carlsson 1991.
17 D'Haenens 1970: 23.
18 Grat, Vielliard & Clémencet 1964.
19 Adigard des Gautries 1954: 422, presents a definition from around 1030 of the toponym *Torhulmus* (old norse *Torholmr*, "l'Île de Thor") from which Tourville-la-Rivière comes: "Insulam super alveum Sequanae quam dicunt nomine Torhulmum, alio quidem vocabulo Oscellum".
20 *Chronicon Fontanallense* 63–91 mentions for August 855 that a small Viking army led by Sydroc took over the *castrum* at *Pistis*, called *Petramamulum*, whose continuity through the Early Middle Ages is established by foundations and Carolingian finds excavated near the present church in Pîtres by Abbé Cochet in 1854.
21 *Annales Bertiniani*, 862, & *Capitularia regnum Francorum*, 864, II, 361.
22 Guillaume de Jumièges, book II, ch. x.
23 *Annales Bertiniani*, 862 & 866.
24 *Annales Bertiniani*, 856.
25 Archives départementales de la Seine-Maritime, under-series 4 SP: *travaux des Ponts et Chaussées sur plages et ports*, & 7 SP: *aménagements des cours d'eau*.
26 Bravard 1996: 171–179.
27 Malandain 1988: 30–45.
28 *Gesta Abbatum Fontanellensium*, 840.
29 Dudon De Saint-Quentin, book II, ch. 11, 44.
30 Follain 1989: 39–78.
31 Bérigny 1926.
32 Morel 1986: 16–29.
33 Rieth 1999.
34 Rieth 1999.
35 Eginhard, ch. 17: 51.
36 Vadstrup 1993: 15–24.
37 *Annales Bertiniani*, 862 & 866.
38 Morcken 1989: 53–78.
39 *Annales Vedastii*, 888, and *Annales Mettenses Priores*, 888.
40 Out of the lower Seine context, *Tellas* is also known as the ancient name of the river Béthune, one of the river Arques' affluents, reaching the Channel at Dieppe.
41 *Annales Bertiniani*, 861.
42 Lair 1897: 3.
43 Vogel 1906: 163, §1.
44 Aimoin, VI: 861.
45 Périn 1990: 168.
46 Arbman & Nilsson 1969: 163–202.
47 Armstrong 1998: 131–164.
48 Abbé Cochet 1871: 87.
49 Elmqvist 1969: 203–224.
50 Abbon, *Bella Parisiacae Urbis*. ed. H. Wacquet, Paris 1964.
51 Shetelig 1954: 67–111.
52 Richards 1999.
53 Périn 1990: 172.
54 Fellows-Jensen 1994: 67–87.
55 Duval 1982.
56 Le Maho 1997: 98.
57 Adigard des Gautries 1954–1955 & 1956–59.
58 Abbé Cochet 1871: 174.
59 Rémy-Watté 1997: 58–63.
60 Dearden 1995.
61 Le Maho 1976: 5–148.
62 In the article quoted above, Jacques Le Maho identified seven main types of fortifications which one may qualify as topographically independent during the ducal period (11th–12th centuries), from the earliest to the latest type: 1) large ring-shaped ramparts, 2) tronconic moated sites, 3) moated sites on promontories, 4) flat and lower moated sites, 5) square moated sites, 6) small ringwalls, and 7) undetermined.
63 Le Maho 1980: 153–165.
64 *Libellus miraculorum S. Bertini*, mai 891.
65 Rogeret 1997: 323.
66 *Libellus miraculorum S. Bertini*, mai 891.
67 Renoux 1982: 327–346.
68 Dudon de Saint-Quentin 1977: 155–156.
69 Guillaume de Jumièges, book II, ch. x.
70 Abbon, *De bello parisiaco*, chant I, v° 174–176.
71 Alpert de Metz, année 884.
72 Biddle & Kjølbye-Biddle 1992: 40.
73 Fournier 1997: 20–21.
74 Skov 1994: 144.
75 Carré & Guillon 1993: 145–158.
76 Birkedal Christensen & Johansen 1992.
77 Ulriksen 1997: 25–41.
78 Le Maho 1994a: 31–33.
79 Dumas-Dubourg 1971.
80 Fauroux 1961.
81 Musset 1985: 113–128.
82 Hérubel 1930.
83 Le Maho 1999.
84 Le Maho 1992: 116–124.
85 *Vita Vulfranni episcopi*, 150–160, ch. VII & IX.
86 Barbé & Barret 1998: 7–50.
87 *Miraculi sancti Eadmundi*, 262, ch. L.
88 Bourgeois 1995: 84–91.
89 Dudon de Saint-Quentin 1979: 155–156 & Guillaume de Jumieges, II, ch. x.
90 Jankuhn (dir.) 1984.

References

Abbon, *Bella parisiacae*. Ed. H. Waquet. *Classiques de l'Histoire de France au Moyen Age* (Paris 1942).

Adigard des Gautries, Jean, "Les noms de personnes scandinaves en Normandie, de 911 à 1066". *Nomina Germanica* 11 (Lund 1954).

— "Les noms de lieux de l'Eure attestés entre 911 et 1066". *Annales de Normandie* (1954–1955).

— "Les noms de lieux de la Seine-Maritime attestés entre 911 et 1066". *Annales de Normandie* (1956–59).

Aimoin de Fleury, *Historia miraculorum et translatorium S. Germani ob irruptionnes Scandinaviannicas*. Ed. Bouquet. A. A., SS, may 861, VI (Paris).

Alpert de Metz, *De diversitate temporum*. Ed. G.H. Pertz. Monumenta Germaniae Historica, SS, anno 884, IV (Hannover-Leipzig 1842), pp. 700–723.

Annales Bertiniani. Ed. F. Grat, J. Vielliard & S. Clémencet (Paris 1964).

Annales Mettenses Priores. Ed. B. von Simson. Monumenta Germaniae Historica SS (Hannover-Leipzig 1905).

Annales Vedastii. Ed. B. von Simson. Monumenta Germaniae Historica SS, II, Rerum Germanicarum (Leipzig-Hannover 1909).

Arbman, Holger, "Fortifications autour de Buchy". *Meddelanden från Lunds Universitets Historiska Museum 1966–1968* (Lund 1969), pp. 41–73.

Arbman, Holger & N.O. Nilsson, "Armes scandinaves de l'époque viking en France". *Meddelanden från Lunds Universitets Historiska Museum 1966–1968* (Lund 1969), pp. 163–202.

Armstrong, S., "Carolingian Coin Hoards and the Impact of the Viking Raids in the Ninth Century". *The Numismatic Chronicle*, CLVIII (London 1998), pp. 131–164.

Barbé, H. & M. Barret, "Aménagement du réseau hydrographique et urbanisation aux abords de l'abbaye St Bertin – Données récentes de l'archéologie à St Omer". *Revue du Nord – Archéologie de la Picardie et du nord de la France 328*, LXXX (Amiens 1998), pp. 7–50.

Bérigny, Charles, *Navigation maritime du Havre à Rouen, ou mémoire sur les moyens de faire remonter jusqu'à Paris tous les bâtimens de mer qui peuvent entrer dans le port du Havre* (Paris 1926).

Biddle, M. & B. Kjølbye-Biddle, "Repton and the Vikings". *Antiquity* LXVI (London 1992), pp. 36–51.

Birkedal Christensen, P. & E. Johansen, "En handelsplads fra yngre jernalder og vikingetid fra Sebbersund". *Aarbøger for Nordisk Oldkyndighed og Historie 1991* (Copenhagen 1992).

Bourgeois, L., "Agglomérations secondaires antiques et noyaux urbains du haut Moyen Age dans l'ouest parisien". In: Cl. Lorren & P. Périn et al., *L'habitat rural du Haut Moyen Age (France, Pays-Bas, Danemark et Grande-Bretagne)*, Mémoires de l'Association Française d'Archéologie Mérovingienne, VI (Rouen 1995), pp. 81–102.

Bravard, J.-P., "Des versants aux cours d'eau, les implications des fluctuations paléohydrologiques à l'époque médiévale". In: M. Colardelle et al., *L'homme et la nature au Moyen-âge, Actes du Vème Congrès International d'archéologie médiévale (Grenoble, 10.6–9.1993)* (Paris 1996), pp. 171–179.

Capitularia regnum Francorum. Ed. A. Boretius & V. Krause. Monumenta Germaniae Historica (Hannover 1883–1897).

Carlsson, D., "Harbours and trading places on Gotland AD 600–1000". In: O. Crumlin-Pedersen et al., *Aspects of Maritime Scandinavia AD 200–1200* (Roskilde 1991).

Carré, Fl. & Guillon, M., "Habitat et nécropole de Portejoie : le site de Tournedos/Val-de-Reuil (Eure), VIIème–XIVème siècles". In: Cl. Lorren & P. Périn et al., *L'habitat rural du Haut Moyen Age (France, Pays-Bas, Danemark et Grande-Bretagne)*, Mémoires de l'Association Française d'Archéologie Mérovingienne, VI (Rouen 1995), pp. 145–158.

Chatellier, P. & L. le Pontois, "La sépulture scandinave à barque de l'Île de Groix". *Bulletin de la Société Archéologique du Finistère*, XXXV (Brest 1908).

Chronicon Fontanallense. Ed. J. Laporte. Société de l'Histoire de Normandie, Mélanges, XV (1951), pp. 63–69.

Cochet, Abbé, *Répertoire Archéologique départemental de la Seine-Inférieure* (Paris 1871).

Crumlin-Pedersen, O., "Søfart og samfund i Danmarks vikingetid". In: P. Mortensen & B.M. Rasmussen et al., *Fra Stamme til Stat i Danmark, 2. Høvdingesamfund & Kongemagt* (Aarhus 1991), pp. 181–208.

Dearden, B.B., "The Ninth-Century Defences of the West Frankish Kingdom against the Vikings in the Light of the Recent Work at Pont-de-l'Arche", Ph.D., Victoria University of Manchester, Department of Archaeology (1995).

D'Haenens, A., *Les invasions Normandes, une catastrophe?* (Paris 1970).

Dudon de Saint-Quentin, *De moribus et actis primorum Scandinavianiae ducum*. Ed. E. Albrectsen (Odense 1979).

Dudonis Sancti Quintini, *De moribus et actis primorum Normanniae ducum*. Ed. J. Lair. Mémoires de la Société

Laurent Mazet-Harhoff

des Antiquaires de Normandie, XXIII (Rouen 1865), pp. 4–314.

Dumas-Dubourg, F., *Le trésor de Fécamp et le monnayage en Francie occidentale pendant la seconde moitié du xème siècle*. Mémoires de la section d'archéologie I (Paris 1971).

Durand, F., *Les Vikings et la Mer* (Paris 1996).

Duval, P.-C., *Le réseau routier antique en Haute-Normandie (nord de la Seine)*, mémoire de maîtrise 1980 (Rouen 1982).

Eginhard, *Vita Karoli*. Ed. Halphen. Classiques de l'Histoire de France (Paris 1947).

Elmqvist, B., "Les fibules de Pîtres". *Meddelanden från Lunds Universitets Historiska Museum 1966–1968* (Lund 1969), pp. 203–224.

Fauroux, M., *Recueil des Actes des Ducs de Normandie de 911 à 1066* (Caen 1961).

Fellows-Jensen, G., "Vikingtidens sted- og personnavne". *Norna-Rapporter* LIV (Uppsala 1994), pp. 67–87.

— "Les noms de lieux d'origine scandinave et la colonisation viking en Normandie. Examen critique de la question". *Proxima Thulé, revue de la Société des études nordiques* (Paris 1994), pp. 63–104.

Follain, E., "Juliobona". *Lillebonne des origines à nos jours*, 39–78 (Saint-Georges-de-Lugançon 1989).

Fournier, P., "Bouafles, Les Mousseaux". *Bilan Scientifique 1996 du Service Régionale de l'Archéologie* (Rouen 1997), pp. 20–21.

Gesta Abbatum Fontanellensium. Ed. F. Lohier & L. Laporte. Société de l'Histoire de Normandie (Rouen-Paris 1936).

Guillaume de Jumièges, *Gesta Scandinaviannorum ducum*. Ed. J. Marx. Société de l'Histoire de Normandie (Rouen-Paris 1914).

Hérubel, M., *Les origines des ports de la Seine-Maritime*. Société d'Edition géographique maritime et coloniale (Le Havre 1930).

Inventio et Miracula Sancti Vulfranni. Trans. J. Laporte. Mélanges de la Société Historique de Normandie (Rouen-Paris 1938).

Jankuhn, H. et al., *Archäologische und naturwissenschaftliche Untersuchungen an ländlichen und früstädtlischen Siedlungen im deutschen Küstengebiet vom 5. Jahrhundert v.Chr. bis zum 11. Jahrhundert n. Chr.* (Bonn 1984).

Lair, J., *Les Scandinaves dans l'île d'Oscelle (855–861)*. Société Historique et Archéologique du Véxin, XX (Paris 1897), pp. 2–39.

Lebecq, S., "Dans l'Europe du Nord des VIIème–IXème siècles, commerce frison ou commerce franco-frison". *Annales* (Lille 1986), pp. 361–377.

Lécolle, F., *Le cours moyen de la Seine au pléistocène moyen et supérieur, géologie et préhistoire* (Rouen 1989).

Le Maho, J., "L'apparition des seigneuries châtelaines dans le Grand-Caux à l'époque ducale". *Archéologie Médiévale*, VI (Caen 1976), pp. 5–148.

— "Les châteaux d'époque franque en Normandie". *Archéologie Médiévale*, X (Caen 1980), pp. 153–165.

— "Note sur l'utilisation de la pierre de Caen dans les églises romanes de la basse vallée de la Seine". *Bulletin de la Commission des Antiquités de la Seine Maritime*, XXXIX (1991) (Rouen 1992), pp. 116–124.

— "Les fouilles de la Cathédrale de Rouen de 1985 à 1993, esquisse d'un premier bilan". *Archéologie Médiévale*, XXIV (Caen 1994), pp. 1–49.

— "Cathédrale Notre-Dame de Rouen, les fouilles de la Cour-des-Maçons de 1991 à 1993". *Rouen et les Vikings, Haute-Normandie Archéologique*, III (Rouen 1994), pp. 61–66.

— "Le haut Moyen Age, l'occupation du sol". In: I. Rogeret et al., *Carte archéologique de la Gaule, la Seine-Maritime 76* (Paris 1997).

— "Les destins comparés de deux cités de fond d'estuaire : Rouen et Nantes, du VIIème au Xème siècle". *Actes du 124ème Congrès des Sociétés Historiques et Scientifiques (Nantes 19–26 avril 1999)* (Nantes 1999).

Libellus miraculorum S. Bertini. Ed. O. Holder-Egger. Monumenta Germaniae Historica, SS, XV (Bonn 1887).

Malandain, J.-J., "La Seine au temps du mascaret". *Chasse-marée*, XXXIV March (Douarnenez 1988), pp. 30–45.

Mazet, L., "Les prémisses maritimes à l'urbanisation du Danemark à l'âge du fer récent (ca. 400ad–1050ad) ; focalisation sur la région du Limfjord". DEA nr. 950085 (unpublished). Supervised by Nils Engberg (Copenhagen) & Jean-François Reynaud (Lyon II) (Lyon 1996).

McGrail, S., "Early Landing Places". In: A.E. Herteig et al., *Conference on Waterfront Archaeology in North European Towns*, II (Bergen 1985).

Miraculi sancti Eadmundi. Ed. F. Liebermann. Ungedruckte anglo-Scandinaviannische Geschichtsquellen (Strasbourg 1879).

Morcken, R., "Old Norse Nautical Distance Tables in the Mediterranean Sea". *The Mariner's Mirror. The International Journal of the Society for Nautical Research*, LXXV (Greenwich 1989), pp. 53–78.

Morel, B., "La gribane de basse Seine". *Chasse-marée*, XXVI (Douarnenez 1986), pp. 16–29.

Musset, L., *Les invasions : Le second assaut contre l'Europe Chrétienne (VIIe–XIe siècles)* (Paris 1964).
— "Les ports en Normandie du xième au xiiième siècle: Esquisse d'histoire institutionnelle". *Cahier des Annales de Normandie*, XVII, pp. 113–128 (Caen 1985).
— "Essai sur le peuplement de la Normandie (vie–xiie siècle)". *Nordica et Normannica, Studia Nordica* 1 (Paris 1997).
Nithard, *Histoire des fils de Louis-le-Pieux*. Ed. P. Lauer. Classiques de l'Histoire de France (Paris, 1926).
Périn, P., "Les objets vikings du Musée des Antiquités de la Seine-Maritime à Rouen". *Recueil d'études en hommage à Lucien Musset, Cahiers des Annales de Normandie*, XXIII (Caen 1990), pp. 161–188.
Rémy-Watté, M., "l'Age du Fer". In: I. Rogeret et al., *Carte archéologique de la Gaule, la Seine-Maritime* 76 (Paris 1997), pp. 58–63.
Renoux, A., "Châteaux Scandinaviands du xème siècle dans le *De moribus et actis primorum Scandinavianniae ducum*, de Dudon de Saint-Quentin". *Mélanges d'archéologie et d'histoire médiévales*, XXVII. Mémoires et Documents, Société de l'Ecole des Chartes (Paris 1982), pp. 327–346.
Richards, J.D., *English Heritage of Viking Age England* (London 1991).
— Heath Wood, Ingleby. Derbyshire, Excavations, July 1998, Interim report (York 1999).
Rieth, E., "La construction médiévale à clin en Normandie: le témoignage du Clos des Galées de Rouen (1293–1418)". In: E. Ridel et al., *L'héritage maritime des Vikings en Europe de l'Ouest, Conference 9.30–3.10.1999 in Flottemanville-Hague* (Caen 2001).
Rogeret, I. et al., *Carte archéologique de la Gaule, la Seine-Maritime* 76 (Paris 1997).
Shetelig, H., "The Viking Graves". *Viking Antiquities in Great Britain and Ireland*, VI (Oslo 1954), pp. 67–111.
Skov, H., "Hustyper i vikingetid og tidlig middelalder. Udvikling af hustyper i det gammeldanske område fra ca. 800–1200 e.Kr.". *Landbebyggelse i middelalderen*. Hikuin XXI (Højbjerg 1994), pp. 139–162.
Ulriksen, J., *Anløbspladser, besejling og bebyggelse i Danmark mellem 200 og 1100 e.Kr.* (Roskilde 1997).
Vadstrup, S., *I vikingernes kølvand* (Roskilde 1993).
Van Heeringen, R.M. et al., *Vroeg-Middeleeuwse ringwalburgen in Zeeland* (Amersfoort 1995).
Vita Vulfranni episcopi. Ed. W. Levison. Monumenta Germaniae Historica, Scriptores rerum Merovingarum, V (Bonn 1995).
Vogel, W., *Die Scandinaviannen und das fränkische Reich bis zur Gründung der Normandie (799–911)*. Heidelberger Abhandlungen zur mittleren und neueren Geschichte, XIV (Heidelberg 1906).
Westerdahl, C., "The maritime cultural landscape". *The International Journal of Nautical Archaeology*, XXII–1 (London 1992), pp. 5–14.

Laurent Mazet-Harhoff

Jens Christian Moesgaard

Vikings on the Continent
The numismatic evidence

During the 9th–11th centuries the Vikings left Scandinavia and went to raid, trade and settle abroad. Raiding of the Carolingian Empire and the states that succeeded it started in the beginning of the 9th century, intensified around the middle of the century and lasted until the first decades of the following century. The Vikings penetrated deep into the country by rivers. Sometimes they stayed in the area for several years, setting up camps for the winter. Groups of Vikings settled in the different locations on a more or less permanent basis. At three different places these settlements were recognised by the local rulers, thus acquiring a more official status. All three places are located in river deltas: of the Rhine, ruled by Vikings from about 850 to 885, of the Loire, conceded at the end of the 9th century and again about 921, and finally of the Seine, given to the chief Rollo about 911. The Vikings were to defend these strategic points against attacks from other Vikings. Only the settlement of the Seine proved long lasting and developed into the powerful duchy of Normandy.

What kind of numismatic evidence can shed light on these invasions and settlements? First of all, the coins struck by the Vikings in the settlements. Second, finds of Viking coins on the Continent. Third, hoards of the specific Viking type reflecting a Viking type economy. Fourth, the more indirect evidence of the impact of the Viking raids on the monetary affairs on the Continent. Finally, the impact in the Viking lands of the looted coins from the Continent.

In the following I will try to give a survey of the available – mostly rather limited – evidence in these fields. It will be necessary to discuss the value of each source within each category of evidence at some length. I will cover the Carolingian Empire (except the Italian parts) during the period of the most intense raiding and settlement: that is, the 9th and the first half of the 10th century.

It is important to bear in mind that the economy of the Northern lands and that of the Empire were very different. The Carolingian Empire had a monetary economy. The coins were counted and used by number at a fixed value per unit generally agreed upon. Foreign coins had to be melted down to be re-struck as domestic coins. The economy of Viking Age Scandinavia – except for Ribe in the 8th century and Hedeby in the 10th – was not a monetary, but a bullion economy. Coins were used along with other items made of precious metals for their metal value by weight. The coins were often bent and pecked to check the quality of the metal, and they were frequently cut into fragments to obtain the appropriate weight for a payment. Most of the coins were foreign: mainly Arabic until *c.* 975 and mainly West European hereafter. The local coin production continued on a rather limited scale until the late 10th century and only dominated the currency from the middle of the 11th century in Denmark, Norway and even later in Sweden. In their settlements in England, the Vikings struck more abundant series of coins in the late 9th and early 10th centuries

Was there an issue of coins by the Vikings in Frisia?

When a chief – Viking or other – acquired a new territory by conquest or treaty, he faced the problem of organising its administration. Should he impose the structures familiar to him from his place of origin or should he build upon the local traditions of his new land? We shall take a look at what the Viking settlers actually did in various territories. In Normandy, we know for sure that the Vikings struck coins. In Frisia, they may have done it. At the Loire delta we have no evidence whatsoever of the Viking coin issues. The alleged Viking issue of Quentovic *c.* 900 is now regarded as an imitative issue struck by the Vikings in England (Grierson & Blackburn 1986: 322 & 616; North 1994: 112)

From around the middle and until the end of the 9th century there was a relatively abundant issue of more or less base gold solidi, imitating the imperial type of Louis the Pious (814–840). On the basis of the find distribution they are traditionally attributed to Frisia. However, quite a few specimens have recently come to light in England, along with a lead trial piece found at Torksey (Lincs.) (pers. inf. M. Blackburn, June 2000). The evidence as it stands at the moment suggests that the coins were struck both in Frisia and in England.

The Vikings settled in Frisia during the period of striking, but it is

Jens Christian Moesgaard

impossible to say whether the issue was controlled by them or by local Frisians. Gold issues were very uncommon at the time; most coins were struck in silver. The imperial prototype for the imitations was a small-scale issue, presumably struck for political prestige of the Emperor, whereas the imitations are more plentiful and seem to have had an economic purpose. Beside Frisia and England, these coins have been found in Norway and in the coastlands of Vendée, south of the Loire delta. Presence of the coins at these sites can be a result of trade, but particularly the coins from Norway could be loot from raiding. The two Vendée coins could also well have been brought there during the raids of the Vikings in the Loire area in the 840s (Grierson 1951; Lebecq 1983: 66–68; Grierson & Blackburn 1986: 329–330; Pagan 1988; Jeanne-Rose 1996: 251).

It has also been suggested that the important mint of Dorestad may have been under Danish control for a while just before its final decline in the middle of the 9th century (Coupland 1988: 21 & 23).

Coin issues in Normandy by the Normans until *c.* 942

We do not know if any coins were issued in Upper Normandy, when the Vikings (hereafter I will call the Vikings settled in Normandy "Normans") arrived in 911/12. It is, however, likely that silver pennies and obols of the type with the monogram of CAROLVS and the inscription + GRATIA DEI REX (the GDR-type), introduced in 864, were still being struck, at least at the main mint in Rouen (dép. Seine-Maritime). However, we would need a well-dated hoard from about that time to be certain.

The numerous GDR-coins of the mints of Bayeux (dép. Calvados) and Curtisasonien (a place whose location is not established, but probably in dép. Orne, Dumas 1971: 106–107; Grierson & Blackburn 1986: 635–637; Dumas & Pilet-Lemière 1989: 125 & 130, note 2) in the hoard of Juaye-Mondaye (dép. Calvados) (Doucet 1879; Duplessy 1985, no. 177), buried about 920, show that these mints were still active just before Middle Normandy was given to the Normans in 924. As for the present day département of La Manche, the western-most part of Normandy, conceded in 933, we have no evidence of the coin production after the scarce GDR-issue of Coutances.

Did the Normans strike coins themselves in Normandy? The first overtly Norman issues are from the reign of William Longsword (927–942),

Fig. 1. Duchy of Normandy, William Longsword (927–942), penny, Rouen. Specimen from the hoard of Terslev, Zealand, Denmark. Royal Coin Cabinet, National Museum, Copenhagen. Enlarged.

son and successor of Rollo. One type carries the name of William on one side and the name of Rouen on the other (Dumas 1979), fig. 1. The other type carries the name of William and title of duke of Brittany (Dolley & Yvon 1971). Whereas the former is straight forward, the latter needs an explanation. Indeed, William wanted to expand into Brittany, but it is unlikely that he ever succeeded in conquering that duchy completely. It is more likely that the title on the coin is a reference to his acquisition in 933 of present day La Manche, which had formerly been a part of Brittany. Coins in the name of William are very rare today, and at the present stage of knowledge one must assume that the issue was rather limited (but a new hoard can change that picture overnight).

Longpérier suggested that the Rouen-coin of William was an imitation of the coins of the pre-Viking East Anglian kings (Longpérier 1870: 83), which carry an image of a cross on both sides, sometimes with crescents in the angles:

Æthelstan I (*c.* 825–845), North 1994, nos. 445–448.

Æthelweard (*c.* 845–855), North 1994, nos. 452–453, especially no. 452 with crescents.

Eadmund (855–869), North 1994, nos. 457–458, especially no. 458 with crescents.

Jens Christian Moesgaard

This suggestion has generally been accepted by later numismatists (Caron 1882: 15–16; Dieudonné 1936: 303; Dumas 1971: 72, note 1; Dumas 1979: 87, note 5; Dhénin 1990: 18). Dumas adds another possible prototype:
Wessex, Æthelwulf (839–858), North 1994, nos. 612–613.

One could add others:
Wessex, Æthelwulf (839–858), North 1994, nos. 603–607.
Kent, Baldred (c. 823–825), North 1994, nos. 213–215.

These coins, though, were more than half a century old, when William started his coinage and they were no longer in circulation in England (Archibald 1988: 273–274). No finds are recorded from France. Thus they were known neither in France nor in England about 930, and only the odd specimen could have been available for copying. This is not very likely and I would prefer to see the Rouen-type as an original, local type.

Were no coins struck by the Normans before William's reign, and was the presumably limited issue under William sufficient to meet the demand for coins at that time? It is impossible to say for certain, but also Carolingian-style coins could have been struck by the Normans during the early decades of their stay in Normandy. The Fécamp (dép. Seine-Maritime) hoard, concealed c. 980/85, contained three low-weight, poor style specimens of the GDR-type from the Bayeux mint. They are not too worn, and they were presumably struck long after the Viking take-over of Middle Normandy in 924, some 60 years before the hoard was buried. They may have been struck during the brief Frankish control of Bayeux 942–945, but they may also be regarded as a purely Norman issue (Dumas 1971: 104–105). On the other hand, the single specimen of the Curtisasonien mint in the same hoard is worn and of the same style as the specimen in the Cuerdale hoard, buried c. 905. Therefore F. Dumas thinks that it was struck long before the burial of the hoard, and that the issue could have been stopped in 924 when the Normans arrived (Dumas 1971: 106–107). The alleged Raoul (923–936) coin of Curtisasonien is a fake (Dumas 1980: 222).

GDR-coins of low weight and bad style, produced by the mint of Rouen, also exist, but none have been recorded in the hoards yet, so it is impossible to date them more precisely.

Yet another coin type is a good candidate of being a Norman issue, even though, once again, we cannot be entirely sure whether it was struck before or after the arrival of the Vikings in Normandy. This is the low weight imitations of the Louis the Pious class 3-coins (reverse legend ChiRhoISTIANA RELIGIO, known as the XR-type, struck *c.* 822–840) with blundered legends, fig. 2, recorded in the following hoards: Coudres (dép. Eure), tentatively dated to 920/23 (Moesgaard 1995: 99), Evreux/Saint-Taurin (dép. Eure), buried about 945 (Duplessy 1985, no. 136) and Haute-Isle (dép. Val-d'Oise), traditionally dated to 898/923 (Duplessy 1985, no. 161). No other finds are known for this type. Its concentration in eastern Normandy and its immediate border areas indicates a Norman origin. The dates would fit to an early Norman issue, but they are not sufficiently precise to ascertain the Viking origin.

The coins surveyed above are all typical for the general monetary evolution of the Carolingian Empire at that time. The royally controlled nation-wide coinage gave way to local coinages. Local types evolved and old traditional Carolingian types were kept ('immobilisation') or imitated. William Longsword was, however, among the very first local magnates to put his name in such a prominent place, omitting all reference to the royal name and title (Dumas 1973). The coin striking of the Normans is thus fully integrated in the local environment. The Vikings used the monetary system they found at their arrival. In this field, they did not bring any traditions from back home.

Finds of Viking coins on the Continent

We have already heard of the finds in Vendée of solidus imitations that may be of Viking origin (see above). There have been recorded scattered finds of other coins struck by the Vikings (see list below) within the borders of the Carolingian Empire. Do they necessarily imply Viking presence? A few coins were possibly brought by individual Vikings who came with either military or peaceful intentions – to raid or to settle. But they could also have come by the usual ways of trade without necessarily involving the Vikings directly. As foreign coins were to be melted down in the regulated monetary system of the Carolingian Empire, the coins that we find today only represent those that escaped the melting pot. We have no means of evaluating the real size of the movement.

The preliminary survey of finds on the Continent of coins struck by the Vikings, presented in the list below, is based on available find inventories

Fig. 2. Normandy? degenerated issue of Louis the Pious, class 3, 10th century. Specimen from the hoard of Evreux/Saint-Taurin (from *Revue Numismatique* 1869–1870). Enlarged.

and should not be regarded as the final checklist. There may well be additional information scattered in excavation reports and local history literature. One should also be aware that in some countries many coin finds are sold directly to collectors without recording. Any information regarding the use of the coins provided by the find spot and archaeological circumstances of the find are thus lost forever. The recording policy is not the same in the various countries covered by the survey, and the results are not directly comparable. In the Netherlands, for instance, coins found by amateur archaeologists with the help of metal detectors are frequently recorded, whereas the French policy of forbidding the use of detectors prevents archaeologists and numismatists from recording the finds made by the amateurs.

The corpus of older finds of coins struck in Scandinavia before *c.* 985 is well established thanks to the research of Brita Malmer (Malmer 1966). Except for a few very late finds in the neighbouring Northern Germany, no finds are recorded on the Continent. This is hardly astonishing, because issues of coins in Scandinavia were rather sparse at that time. Finds of these coins are very rare even in England, which, in comparison to the Continent, was subjected to more intensive Viking influence (Archibald 1991).

Issues made by the Vikings in England are more plentiful (North 1994, nos. 463–557), but only a few specimens have been found on the Continent. In France, the two only finds are from Brittany. Were these coins brought to Brittany by the Vikings? After all, the Vikings settled for a while at the Loire delta and in the southern Breton coastlands. Nevertheless, one should note that non-Viking English coins dated to the Viking period were also found in France (Duplessy 1985, nos. 123ter, 137, 267; Dolley & Yvon 1971; Völckers 1965, XXIV, 114–116; Jeanne-Rose 1996, no. 117; Haertle 1997, no. 51/93; unpublished lunette-coin from the excavations at the construction of the metro in Rouen). The Viking coins mark no increase compared to the general flow of non-Viking English coins. The English coins in general only count for a minor part of the coin finds from the period. Moreover, the Rennes hoard is clearly a typical Carolingian hoard, so at least the last owner of the Saint Edmund coins contained in it would not have been a Viking. It has even been suggested that this hoard belonged to the monks of the Saint-Melaine Monastery, who concealed it while preparing to flee a Viking attack (Chédeville & Guillotel 1984: 384). The Viking coins could well have come to Brittany by way of ordinary trade with England without any particular Viking involvement as pointed out by Anne Nissen-Jaubert with reference to the coin from Camp de Péran (Nissen-Jaubert 1988: 235).

In the Netherlands, a few single finds of coins from the early 10th century are recorded. They are from the present day province called Noord-Holland, which was under Viking rule until 885 (Besteman 1997: 200–201). Thus, by the time the coins were lost, the Viking rule was over; but maybe some settlers remained and kept contact with the York Vikings? It is impossible to say, and the coins may well have arrived by ordinary trade.

There was a massive export of silver dirhems struck in the silver-producing areas in Central Asia via the Russian rivers to the Baltic area, and thousands of coins have been found in the countries around the Baltic Sea. Therefore, finds in Western Europe of Arabic coins struck in the Middle East and Central Asia (but not in Spain or North Africa) might be considered as indirect proof of the Viking influence. Some of the coins possibly came there by a transit route through Scandinavia or the Slavic lands near the Baltic Sea. However, other coins may have come through an alternative inland route via Prague, which is well documented (Lotter 1993). Islamic coins from Spain or North Africa are rare in Scandinavia (Kromann 1988; Mikolajczyk 1988). Therefore finds of such coins in Western Europe probably have nothing to do with the Vikings.

Older finds of dirhems are well-documented thanks to a survey by Duplessy in 1956, which shows that dirhems were relatively rare in the Carolingian Empire. Moreover, several of them are of North African or Spanish origin and must have come to the Empire directly over the Pyrenees or the Mediterranean rather than through Scandinavia (Duplessy 1956, finds nos. 3–5, 8–11, 13–14, 25. No. 11 was found in Wiesbaden-Biebrich,

Jens Christian Moesgaard

see Völckers 1965, XLII, 48). More coins have been found since 1956 (see for instance Blackburn 1993: 49, nos. 17–18; Coupland 1997), but they do not really change the picture obtained by Duplessy. One exception is, perhaps, the two dirhems from Wieringen (prov. Noord-Holland), which was, as we have seen, an area under Viking rule (Besteman 1997: 215).

From the travel journal of a 10th-century Arabic traveller we know that there were eastern dirhems, struck in Samarqand in 913/14 and 914/15, circulating in Mainz (Hatz & Linder Welin 1968: 29, note 114). On the other hand, coins struck in Spain were used as prototypes (Hatz & Linder Welin 1968: 13–16) for issues of imitations of Arabic coins at the time of Emperor Henry II (1014–1024).

The overall picture of the Arabic coins in the Carolingian Empire and its successor states is that coins from Spain and North Africa were at least as numerous as the Eastern coins. Thus it seems that the Vikings only played a limited role in the import of Arabic silver to the Empire.

All in all only six English Viking coins, a few dirhems and maybe two imitations of solidi can be related to the Vikings in one way or another. This is not much compared to the hundreds and thousands of local coins found in the Empire. Of course this list of finds does not give a real measure of the importance of import of Viking coins, because, as mentioned above, foreign coins were melted down to be re-struck as domestic coins. The only area that really stands out is Noord-Holland. In contrast it should be noted that none have been found in the Viking colony of Normandy.

Evidence of the bullion economy within the Empire

The hoards of the Viking lands are very characteristic. They consist of a mixture of coins of different origins, often bent and pecked in order to check the quality of the metal and sometimes cut into small fragments. They also contain silver lingots and jewellery, likewise cut into fragments. This reflects the bullion economy (see above). On the contrary, the Carolingian Empire and the Anglo-Saxon Kingdoms had a monetary type of economy (see above). Here the hoards are made up only of coins of local origin, whole and without pecks.

A massive appearance of pecked, bent and fragmented coins in hoards and/or as single finds within an area would mean that the Vikings had introduced a bullion economy in that area. Several finds of this type exist in

Fig. 3. Charles the Bald, class 2, 864–875/7, penny, Rouen (Musée des Antiquités, Rouen. Photo: Y. Deslandes).

Fig. 4. Degenerated issue of Charles the Bald's penny struck in Rouen. This specimen carries one peck on the reverse (Musée des Antiquités, Rouen. Photo: Y. Deslandes). For the prototype issue, see fig. 3.

the Danelaw, but it does not seem to be the case on the Continent. To my knowledge only two Viking-type hoards (mixed coins, lingots, and jewellery, bent and cut) are recorded. The first was found in 1996 in Westerklief in Wieringen Parish with the help of a metal detector (prov. Noord-Holland, Netherlands). The hoard, which can be dated to about 850 on the grounds of the numismatic evidence, contained jewellery, lingots and coins. Many items are of south Scandinavian origin. The find spot is within the very area under Viking rule from about 850 to 885, and it is likely that contents of the hoard belonged to a Viking settler (Besteman 1996, 1997; Coupland 1997). In 1999 a new hoard of hack silver and Arabic and Carolingian coins was found at Westerklief, near the find spot of the first hoard of 1996. It is currently being studied by Arent Pol and Jan Besteman (pers. inf. Arent Pol, Dec. 1999). Nevertheless, Ralf Wiechmann suggests that a mixed hoard can exist in the periphery of the Empire without any specific Viking connection. He quotes as an example the Krinkberg/Pöschendorf hoard (Wiechmann 1996: 127) and points out that the mixed Ilanz (Switzerland, Völckers 1965: 73–79) hoard cannot possibly be connected with the Vikings (Wiechmann, pers. inf., March 2000).

There are a few other hoards with jewellery, for instance Féchain (dép. Nord, France) (Dhénin 1985) and Roermond (prov. Limburg, Netherlands) (Gelder 1985), or with lingots – like Molliens-Vidame (dép. Somme, France) (Duplessy 1985, no. 216); but none of them have the specific mixed composition typical for the Viking hoards.

As for the pecking, one unpublished coin from the collection of the

Jens Christian Moesgaard

Musée départemental des Antiquités de la Seine-Maritime in Rouen seems to have got one single peck. It is a degenerated specimen of the GDR-type in the name of Charles, struck at the mint of Rouen, fig. 3–4:

> Obv. x CRATIA RI RE+ (legend starts at 3h) – retrograde CAROLVS monogram.
> Rev. + ROTVMACVZ CIVII (legend starts at 11h30) – cross.
> Silver; 1.23g; die axis 0h30; secondary treatment: peck in the second quarter of the reverse cross.
> Musée départemental des Antiquités de la Seine-Maritime, inv. 94.5.2.

Unfortunately, the find spot of this coin has not been recorded. It was acquired in 1994 from the heirs of a collector from Rouen. This collector had bought coins both locally and from dealers. But as the coin is not very impressive and the collector was interested in all kinds of coins and not particularly in coins from the Rouen mint, which she was unlikely to have ordered from afar, a local Norman provenance is likely, even if it cannot be proved. If indeed this coin was circulated and pecked in Normandy, we have the first example of a coin that was demonstratively used by a Viking in Normandy.

Pecking has, as far as I know, never been noted on any other coin found in the Empire. The odd specimen might have been neglected by scholars, but if the phenomenon had been wide-spread, it would have been noted by numismatists and archaeologists.

The scarcity of the Viking related coin finds is yet another clue to the quick assimilation of the Viking settlers in Normandy.

Impact of the Viking raids on the monetary affairs on the Continent

The flow of silver towards Scandinavia due to raiding and tributes had an impact on the monetary affairs of the Carolingian Empire and its successor states. Indeed, during the period 840–864, the tight central control of coinage was largely loosened. The nation-wide unity of weight and type broke down. The weight standard and alloy diminished, which may be a result of the dearth of silver after the Viking raiding, but Arabic attacks and civil unrest should also be taken into account (Coupland 1991a: 152–155). The more spectacular is therefore the success of the reinforcement of the rules regarding silver content and new uniformity of type ordered in 864. Control of coinage lasted for a few more decades until the centrifugal force of early feudalism put an end to centralised nation-wide coinage (Dumas 1973). But this was a general trend in society, and not a direct result of Viking activity.

Some scholars have dealt with particular aspects that will be summarised below. Grierson has suggested that striking of the GDR-type, introduced in 864, was largely intensified in 866 in order to pay a huge tribute to the Vikings agreed upon that year. The edict ordering the new issue in 864 explicitly limited the number of mints to 10, but we know of over a hundred mints participating in this issue, of which many never struck other issues and only had a very limited output. Numismatists have tried to explain these features in different ways; however, Grierson's hypothesis would solve the problem: the extra mints were opened only for a short while in 866 to turn big amounts of plate into coins very rapidly in order to pay off the Vikings (Grierson 1990). Of course, this hypothesis suggests that the tributes were paid in coins and not in plate as usually assumed (Hatz & Jonsson 1976: 28–29) and, furthermore, that the Vikings melted the coins down again because as we shall see below the GDR-coins are not common in the Scandinavian finds.

It has been generally assumed that the increase in the number of hoards in France in the second half of the 9th century was a direct consequence of fear for Viking attacks. However, Armstrong's excellent survey of all known French hoards from the 9th century clearly demonstrates that there is no general geographic correlation between known Viking attacks and hoard find spots. Thus fear for the Viking invasions cannot solely explain all hoards. Carolingian civil wars and ordinary hiding of savings in a society that had no banks were also responsible for many of them. Armstrong suggests that many hoards were hidden in an attempt to avoid paying the heavy taxes for the *Danegeld*. If this is correct, the hoards are indirect evidence of the disarray caused by the Vikings (Armstrong 1998).

It is difficult to establish precisely a deposit date for any particular hoard and to be sure that this hoard has a connection to any recorded attack nearby. It is, however, plausible to explain a certain number of hoards in terms of fear of Viking attacks. Armstrong discusses this in detail, so I will only give a few examples here. The hoards of Compiègne (dép. Oise, France) and Féchain (dép. Nord, France) end with coins of Eudes (887–898) and it seems reasonable to assume a connection with the raiding and temporary settlement of the Vikings in this area during the years 889–891 (Dhénin 1985 & 1997: 312). The hoard of Hénouville (dép. Seine-Maritime, France) in the lower Seine valley deposited around 825/50 may well have been hidden by someone experiencing the first Viking raid on the Seine in 841 (Moesgaard 1997). The find spot is on the top of the slope, which gives a good view over the river with the advancing ships.

Particular features make it plausible to connect some hoards with the Viking raids. The Burgundian hoards of Issy-l'Evêque and 'near Autun' (dép. Saône-et-Loire, France) may be parcels of one single hoard (Duplessy 1985, nos. 172 & 23; Haertle 1997, nos. 59 & 70). They have a very high proportion of coins from Curtisasonien and Lisieux in Lower Normandy, which are several hundred kilometres away from the find spot. They contain only a small amount of the local Burgundian coins of Autun and Nevers. This composition is very unusual because coins from Neustria did not normally circulate in big numbers in Burgundy (Metcalf 1990). It has been suggested that this hoard may represent savings of a refugee from the Viking invasion, fleeing insecure Neustria for inland Burgundy (Grierson & Blackburn 1986: 636; see also Metcalf 1990: 80). The dating of this hoard (these hoards) is much debated. It must be placed after 875 because it contains the imperial issue of Nevers. A more precise date depends on the date assigned to the coins of Saint-Nazaire-d'Autun. Some authors attribute them to the GDR-issue of Charles the Bald struck in 864–875/77 (Grierson & Blackburn 1986: 542; Haertle 1997, nos. 59 & 70), others to Carloman (882–884) (Duplessy 1985, nos. 172 & 23), and, finally, some to Charles the Simple (898–922) (Morrison & Grunthal 1967: 298; Armstrong 1998: 164).

Impact of the loot in coins from the Continent in the Viking lands

This is not the place to discuss in detail some very complex problems in connection with the import of the Continental coins to Scandinavia in the 9th century (Coupland 1991b; Metcalf 1996: 422–428). Only a broad overview will be given and a few phenomena will then be discussed.

Finds of Carolingian coins in Scandinavia are relatively rare. The most common types are the XR-type of Louis the Pious, struck *c.* 822–840, and the Cologne and Strasbourg issues of the early 10th century. Many specimens are pierced and looped for use as jewellery. Finds exist in all three Scandinavian countries, but the majority is from Denmark (including Scania). Many coins appear in 10th- and even 11th-century hoards (Galster 1959; Bendixen 1988; Skaare 1966; Skaare 1976: 43–47; Hatz & Jonsson 1976: 28–29; Coupland 1991b).

The scarcity is remarkable in the light of the evidence of chroniclers who tell us about huge amounts of tribute paid to the Vikings. It is even more noticeable compared to the amount of contemporary and slightly later Arabic coins found in Sweden (they are much rarer in Norway and Denmark during the 9th century). On purely numismatic grounds one would never have imagined that Scandinavia's contacts with Western Europe were as important as its contacts with Central Asia. Many explanations have been suggested for this apparent paradox. Some scholars have suggested that the Vikings spent the booty before going home or brought it to England rather than to Scandinavia. Another explanation is that coins were melted down and turned into ingots, plate or jewellery either before arriving in Scandinavia or in Scandinavia itself. The dirhems would have survived, at least in the 10th century, because they fitted into the predominant weight standard used in the bullion economy (Coupland 1991b). One could also look at the big silver production of the Central Asian mines, which was turned into coins and exported. In the framework of this explanation, coin import reflects flows of metal from production areas rather than booty.

Even so, the issue of Charlemagne in Dorestad became the prototype of one of the first Scandinavian issues, which took place in Hedeby in the 9th century. At a first glance, this seems strange because no such coin has been found in Scandinavia, but in fact the Hedeby-issue did not imitate the prototype directly. It is an imitation of an imitation, struck in East Frisia neighbouring Scandinavia (Malmer 1966).

The import of German coins dated to the 10th and the 11th centuries went on a much larger scale. The opening of the very active Saxon silver mines explains why Arabic coins were replaced by German ones. In the last quarter of the 10th century and the first half of the 11th century, German coins formed about a half of the currency, supplemented by English and local Scandinavian coins. The hoards usually consist of a mixture of English and German coins of various origin, and it has been suggested that this was

Jens Christian Moesgaard

Fig. 5. Duchy of Normandy, Monastery of Saint-Ouen, penny, c. 940, Rouen. Specimen from the hoard of Terslev, Zealand, Denmark (Royal Coin Cabinet, National Museum, Copenhagen). Enlarged.

Fig. 6. Duchy of Normandy, Richard I (942/45–996), penny, Rouen. Specimen from the hoard of Vålse, Falster, Denmark (Royal Coin Cabinet, National Museum, Copenhagen). Enlarged.

the result of the monetary stock available to Northern German merchants, and thus rather a result of trading than of raiding (Jonsson 1990 & 1993).

Finds of coins struck in Normandy by the descendants of the Vikings are rare in Scandinavia as well. Only three 10th-century coins are known from present day Denmark (Dumas 1979, finds 14 and 16; Galster 1959: 74, no. 48 & p. 77; Coupland 1991b: 12; Moesgaard 2000) (figs. 1, 5–6). Seventeen late 10th- and 11th-century coins are known from Sweden (Dumas 1979, find 37; Hatz 1989; Golabiewski Lannby 1992: 245; Moesgaard 2000). This is not much compared to the bulk of German coins, especially when one knows that at least sporadic contacts between Scandinavia and Normandy were kept throughout the 10th century. Once again, the finds rather reflect the inflow from a silver producing area (Germany) than regular contacts.

Particular hoards have been seen as booty from raiding. Approximately 1000 Carolingian coins from the Cuerdale hoard (Lancashire, UK), that belongs to the Viking type, have traditionally been seen as booty from the two raids on the Continent. A parcel of 900 coins from the Loire Valley/Aquitaine region dating from the mid-890s (898) and another of approximately 100 coins from the Netherlands, dating from around 902 (Graham-Campbell 1992: 10). A distinctive Viking feature of the Cuerdale coins is the pecking, i.e. test-marks of the quality of the silver made with a knife. It is assumed that the number of pecks on any individual coin is a measure of the length of its circulation among Vikings. It turned out that pecking is consistent within both parcels, older coins being on average as pecked as earlier ones. The theory of booty from two expeditions is thus confirmed by a refined analysis (M. Archibald, pers. inf., June 2000, contra Archibald 1990: 18 & 1992: 17–18).

Besides a bulk of fragments of the Arabic dirhems, a recently discovered hoard, deposited in the 940s at Grisebjerggård, Boeslunde parish, south-west Zealand, contains several Nordic, English and Carolingian coins. The latter form a homogeneous parcel of early 10th-century coins of the mints of Bruges, Tournai and Cologne. Would this be the booty from a raid in the lower Rhine? Identification and analysis of this hoard by Gert Rispling and the author of this article is not yet finished, so it is too early to say.

Some other hoards stand out due to their exceptionally homogeneous content, like the Kättilstorp (Västergötland, Sweden) and Mullaghboden (Kildare, Ireland) hoards from the early years of the reign of Charles the Bald (840–877) which contain parcels of coins from Melle and Poitiers. This could be booty from a raid on Poitou (Coupland 1991a: 133). The Häljarp hoard (Scania, Sweden) contains a parcel of 30 coins of Louis the Pious (814–840) of which several are presumed to be from southern France (Coupland 1991b: 20–21, 25; Metcalf 1996: 425). This shows what kinds of coins the Vikings got hold of abroad, before they were melted down.

The Vikings were also interested in the expertise that they found on the Continent. The coins struck by the Vikings in East Anglia and the Southern Danelaw *c.* 895–*c.* 917 in the name of Saint Edmund carry the name of a moneyer on the reverse. Of the approximately 80 recognisable names, no

Jens Christian Moesgaard

less than 60 plus are continental. This is a much higher proportion than in any Anglo-Saxon coinage. Were these people brought to England by the Vikings as skilled experts (Smart 1985)? Unless they were forced, this implies close and peaceful contacts with the Frankish society. Moreover, some types and legends on Viking coins struck in England imitate Carolingian types (North 1994: 106–116; Grierson & Blackburn 1986: 321–322)

Conclusion

The present paper has examined different categories of numismatic evidence of the presence of Vikings on the Continent.

As for the organised Viking settlements the picture is diverse. There are several finds that are tentatively attributed to a known settlement in the Rhine delta: two hoards of the Viking type and stray finds of dirhems. In the aftermath some Viking coins from England also came to this area. The hoards must have had Viking owners, but it is not impossible that the stray finds represent objects that were lost by non-Vikings who had acquired them through trade. The mere concentration in the province of Noord-Holland indicates, nevertheless, that there is a relation between these finds and the Viking presence. Frisia had a specific gold issue at that time, but it is impossible to say whether it was made by Viking invaders or by local Frisians.

In Normandy, only few Viking related coin finds have been recorded. The coin issues by the Vikings are in a purely late Carolingian/early feudal tradition. This is evidence of the quick assimilation of the Viking invaders.

In the Loire delta settlement no Viking coins have so far been found. In the broader area a few English Viking coins and some Frisian gold coins have been found. At least three English Viking coins were found in a hoard that was clearly owned by a local man.

Is this picture true, or is the difference between Frisia and the two other settlements caused by the modern practice of recording the finds? Indeed, finds made with the help of metal detectors are recorded in the Netherlands, whereas the French policy of interdiction makes it impossible to declare coins found by amateur archaeologists with the help of detectors. Our knowledge of the Viking occupation of several areas in England and the Netherlands has changed most dramatically in recent years due to the finds made with the help of metal detectors (Besteman 1997; Margeson 1996;

Denison 1999; Archibald 1999). Maybe the same will happen in Normandy if the policy is changed.

Numismatic evidence of raiding outside the settlements is sparse. Viking activity is not solely responsible for the increase in the hiding of hoards in the 9th century. Civil unrest also has its share. Maybe some hoards reflect attempts at tax evasion, when heavy taxes were levied on the population in order to pay tribute to the Vikings. The outflow of silver for tribute and as booty from Viking looting would have affected the stock of the precious metals and thus the currency, but this is not yet fully elucidated. The period 840–64 saw an unstable monetary situation, which may be a result of Viking raids. One very important Carolingian issue (the GDR) may have been launched in order to get enough coins to pay tribute to the Vikings, but the scarcity of the Carolingian coin finds in Scandinavia rather indicates the use of other means of payment than coins.

A preliminary check-list of finds of Viking coins (9th–10th centuries) in the Carolingian Empire

France
Rennes (dép. Ille-et-Vilaine), hoard buried 920/23, 136 coins.
East Anglia/Southern Midlands, St Edmund Memorial, late issue without pellets, North 1994, no. 483, *c.* 905–910, 3 specimens, moneyers Winie, "Clarius" and "Adfbn".
Lafaurie 1965: 304–305, nos. 134–136.

Plédran (dép. Côtes-d'Armor), single find from the excavation of the fortified site of Camp de Péran.
York, St. Peter, phase 2, *c.* 910–*c.* 920, North 1994, no. 553 (identified as phase 2 because of its poor style; the weight is not mentioned).
Nissen-Jaubert 1988: 234–235 & 236, fig. 4.

Netherlands
Egmond (prov. Noord-Holland), single find.
East Anglia/Southern Midlands, St Edmund Memorial, *c.* 895–*c.* 910,

moneyer Adradus, has been mounted, North 1994, no. 483.
Pol 1993, no. 49

Heemskerk (prov. Noord-Holland), single find.
East Anglia/Southern Midlands, St Edmund Memorial, *c.* 895–*c.* 910, North 1994, no. 483.
Pol 1993, no. 57

Germany
Dietrichsfeld (Kreis Aurich, Ostfriesland), hoard buried 1010/50, 439 coins, jewellery.
22 pre-1000 Nordic coins.
Malmer 1966: 260, no. 1 & p. 231, tab. 35.

Lienen (Kreis Wesermarsch, Oldenburg), hoard, partially recorded, buried some time after 938, only 2 coins examined.
At least one Nordic Carolus-imitation. Malmer CEIIIA1/DIIIA2, KG7, *c.* 900–*c.* 950.
Malmer 1966: 260, no. 2 & p. 202, tab. 33.

Note

This article was submitted in 2000. It has not been updated. Since then, I have published "Monnaies normandes dans les regions baltiques à l'époque viking" in *Revue Numismatique* (2005), pp. 123–144, "Les Vikings en Bretagne d'après les monnaies" in *Bulletin de la Société française de numismatique* (2006), pp. 131–139, and "A Survey of Coin Production and Currency in Normandy, 864–945" in James Graham-Campbell & Gareth Williams (eds), *Silver Economy in the Viking Age* (Walnut Creek, 2007), pp. 99–121. I am preparing an updated survey of Carolingian coins found in Denmark, as well as an account of the first Viking hoard in France, which appeared in early 2007 at Saint-Pierre-des-Fleurs in Normandy.

References

Archibald, M., "English medieval coins as dating evidence". In: J. Casey & R. Reece (eds), *Coins and the Archaeologist*. 2nd ed. (London 1988), pp. 264–301.

— "Pecking and bending: the evidence of British finds". In: B. Malmer & K. Jonsson (eds), *Sigtuna Papers* (Stockholm 1990), pp. 11–24.

— "Against the tide: coin-movement from Scandinavia to the British Isles in the Viking Age". *NNF-Nytt*, no. 1 (1991), pp. 19–22.

— "Dating Cuerdale: The Evidence of the Coins". In: J. Graham-Campbell (ed.), *Viking Treasure from the North West* (Liverpool 1992), pp. 15–20.

— "Two Ninth-Century Viking Weights found near Kingston, Dorset". *The British Numismatic Journal* 68 (1998), pp. 11–20.

Armstrong, S., "Carolingian Coin Hoards and the Impact of the Viking Raids in the Ninth Century". *Numismatic Chronicle* 158 (1998), pp. 131–164.

Bendixen, K., "Nyere danske fund af merovingiske, karolingiske og ældre danske mønter". In: P. Berghaus et al. (eds), *Commentationes Numismaticae 1988, Festgabe für Gert und Vera Hatz* (Hamburg 1988), pp. 37–50.

Besteman, J.C., *Vikingen in Noord-Holland?* (Harleem 1996).

— "De vondst van Westerklief, gemeente Wieringen: Een zilverschat uit de vikingperiode". *Oudheidkundige Mededelingen uit het Rijksmuseum van Oudheiden te Leiden* 77 (1997), pp. 199–226.

Blackburn, M., "Coin circulation in Germany during the early Middle Ages, the evidence of single finds". In: B. Kluge (ed), *Fernhandel und Geldwirtschaft* (Sigmaringen 1993), pp. 37–54.

Boeles, P.C.J.A., "Les trouvailles de monnaies carolingiennes dans les Pays-Bas, spécialement celles des trios provinces septentrionales". *Jaarboek voor Munten Penningkunde* (1915), pp. 1–98.

Caron, E., *Monnaies féodales françaises* (Paris 1882).

Chédeville, A. & H. Guillotel, *La Bretagne des saints et des rois ve–xe siècle* (Rennes 1984).

Coupland, S., "Dorestad in the Ninth Century. The Numismatic Evidence". *Jaarboek voor Munt- en Penningkunde* 75 (1988), pp. 5–26.

— 1991a. "The Early Coinage of Charles the Bald, 840–864". *Numismatic Chronicle* 151 (1991), pp. 121–158.

— 1991b. "Carolingian Coinage and Scandinavian Silver". *Nordisk Numismatisk Årsskrift* 1985–86 (1991), pp. 11–32.

— 1997. [Review of Besteman 1996]. *Numismatic Chronicle* (1997), pp. 273–274.

Denison, S., "History from fields and back gardens". *British Archaeology* 46 (July 1999), pp. 6–7.

Dhénin, M., "Bijoux et trésor monétaire argent". In: P. Périn & L.-C. Feffer (eds), *La Neustrie* (Rouen 1985), pp. 416–419.

— "Les monnaies normandes". *Les conférences d'histoire locale du lycée de Domfront* 9 (1990), pp. 14–30.

— "Monnaies des fouilles de la Place des Hallettes à Compiègne (Oise)". *Revue archéologique de Picardie, no. spécial 13* (1997), pp. 309–315.

Dieudonné, A. Manuel de numismatique française, IV, *Monnaies féodales françaises* (Paris 1932).

Dolley, M. & J. Yvon., "A Group of Tenth-century Coins found at Mont-Saint-Michel". *British Numismatic Journal* 40 (1971), pp. 1–16.

Doucet, L. "Notice sur des monnaies Carlovingiennes trouvées à Juaye-Mondaye, arrondissement de Bayeux (Calvados), en 1870". In: *Mémoires de la Société d'agriculture, sciences et belles lettres de Bayeux* 9 (1879/82), pp. 215–258.

Dumas Dubourg, F., *Le trésor de Fécamp et le monnayage en Francie occidentale pendant la seconde moitié du xe siècle* (Paris 1971).

— "Le début de l'époque féodale en France d'après les monnaies". *Bulletin du Cercle d'Etudes Numismatiques* (Brussels 1973), pp. 65–77.

— "Les monnaies normandes". *Revue Numismatique* (1979), pp. 84–140.

— "Les monnaies de Raoul, roi de France (923–936)". In: *Mélanges de numismatique, d'archéologie et d'histoire offert à Jean Lafaurie* (Paris 1980), pp. 215–222.

Dumas, F. & J. Pilet-Lemière, "La monnaie normande – xe–xiie siècle". In: H. Galinié (ed.), *Les mondes Normands* (Caen 1989), pp. 125–131.

Duplessy, J., "La circulation des monnaies arabes en Europe occidentale du viiie au xiiie siècles". *Revue Numismatique* (1956), pp. 101–163.

— *Les trésors monétaires médiévaux et modernes découverts en France, I (751–1223)* (Paris 1985).

Galster, G., "Carolingian Coins found in Denmark". *Coins and History* (Copenhagen 1959), pp. 65–78 (Danish version in *Nordisk Numismatisk Årsskrift* [1951]).

Gelder, H.E. van, "Coins from Dorestad, Hoogstraat I". In: W.A. van Es & W.J.H. Verwers (eds), *Excavations in Dorestad*

Jens Christian Moesgaard

I: *The Habour. Hoogstraat 1* (Amersfoort 1980), pp. 212–224.

— "De Karolingische muntvondst Roermond". *Jaarboek voor Munt- en Penningkunde* 72 (1985), pp. 13–49.

Gilles, K.-J., "Neuere karolingische Münzfunde aus Trier". *Funde und Ausgrabungen im Bezirk Trier* 14 (Trier 1982), pp. 24–29.

— "Eine karolingisch-ottonische Münzfälscherwerkstatt in Trier? Nachträge bzw Ergänzungen zum Katalog der merowingischen und karolingischen Fundmünzen". *Funde und Ausgrabungen im Bezirk Trier* 15 (Trier 1983), pp. 35–42.

— "Fundmünzen der sächsischen Kaiserzeit aus dem Trier Land". *Funde und Ausgrabungen im Bezirk Trier* 17 (Trier 1985), pp. 40–47.

Golabiewski Lannby, M., "The Royal Coin Cabinet, Stockholm 1990". *Nordisk Numismatisk Årsskrift* (1991), pp. 245–255.

Graham-Campbell, J., "The Cuerdale Hoard: a Viking and Victorian Treasure". In: J. Graham-Campbell (ed.), *Viking Treasure from the North West. The Cuerdale Hoard in its Context* (Liverpool 1992), pp. 1–14.

Grierson, P., "The Gold Solidus of Louis the Pious and its Imitations". *Jaarboek voor Munt- en Penningkunde* 38 (1951), pp. 1–41 (reprinted with additions in *Dark Age Numismatics* [London 1979]).

— "The 'Gratia dei rex' Coinage of Charles the Bald". In: M.T. Gibson & J.L. Nelson (eds), *Charles the Bald: Court and Kingdom*. 2nd ed. (London 1990), pp. 52–64.

Grierson, P. & M. Blackburn, *Medieval European Coinage*, vol. 1, *The Early Middle Ages (5th–10th centuries)* (Cambridge 1986).

Haeck, A., *Middeleeuwse muntschatten gevonden in België (750–1433)* (Brussels 1996).

Haertle, C. M., *Karolingische Münzfunde aus dem 9. Jahrhundert*, 2 vols (Cologne 1997).

Hatz, V., "Die französischen Münzen des 10./11. Jahrhunderts in den schwedischen Funden der Wikingerzeit". In: U. Ehrenvärd et al. (eds), *Festskrift till Lars O. Lagerqvist* (Stockholm 1989), pp. 121–129.

Hatz, V. & U.S. Linder Welin, "Deutsche Münzen des 11. Jahrhunderts nach byzantinisch-arabischem Vorbild in den schwedischen Funden der Wikingerzeit". *Commentationes de nummis saeculorum IX–XI in Suecia repertis* 2 (Stockholm 1968), pp. 1–38.

Hatz, G. & K. Jonsson, "Vikingatidens myntimport". *Kulturhistorisk Leksikon for nordisk middelalder*, vol. 20, cols. 25–35 (Copenhagen 1976).

Ilisch, P., *Münzfunde und Geldumlauf in Westfalden in Mittelalter und Neuzeit* (Münster 1980).

— *Münzfunde in Ostwestfalen, Mittelalter und Neuzeit* (Münster 1992).

Jeanne-Rose, O., "Trouvailles isolées de monnaies carolingiennes en Poitou: inventaire provisoire". *Revue Numismatique* (1996), pp. 241–283.

Jonsson, K., "The import of German coins to Sweden and Denmark c.920–990". In: K. Jonsson & B. Malmer (eds), *Sigtuna Papers* (Stockholm 1990), pp. 139–143.

— "The routes for the importation of German and English coins to the Northern Lands in the Viking Age". In: B. Kluge (ed.), *Fernhandel und Geldwirtschaft* (Sigmaringen 1993), pp. 205–232.

Kromann, A., "Finds of Iberian Islamic coins in the northern lands". In: M.G. Marques & D.M. Metcalf (eds), *Problems of Medieval Coinage in the Iberian Area* (Santarém 1988), pp. 243–253.

Lafaurie, J., "Deux trésors carolingiens: Saumeray (Eure-et-Loir), Rennes (Illeet-Vilaine)". *Revue Numismatique* (1965), pp. 262–305.

Lebecq, S., *Marchands et navigateurs frisons de Haut Moyen Age*, vol. 1 (Lille 1983).

Longpérier, A. de, "Louis d'Outremer en Normandie. Trouvaille d'Evreux". *Revue Numismatique* (1869/70), pp. 71–85.

Lotter, F., "Die Juden zwischen Rhein und Elbe im Zeitalter Bernwards von Hildesheim". In: *Bernward von Hildesheim und das Zeitalter der Ottonen, Katalog der Ausstellung*, Hildeheim, vol. 1 (1993), pp. 225–230.

Malmer, B., *Nordiska Mynt före år 1000* (Lund 1966).

Margeson, S., "Viking Settlement in Norfolk: A Study of New Evidence". In: S. Margeson, B. Ayres & S. Heywood (eds), *A Festival of Norfolk Archaeology* (Norwich 1996), pp. 47–57.

Metcalf, D.M., "A sketch of the currency in the time of Charles the Bald". In: M.T. Gibson & J.L. Nelson (eds), *Charles the Bald: Court and Kingdom*. 2nd ed. (London 1990), pp. 65–97.

— "Viking-Age Numismatics 2. Coinage in the Northern Lands in Merovingian and Carolingian Times". *Numismatic Chronicle* (1996), pp. 399–428.

Mikolajczyk, A., "Movements of Spanish Umayyad dirhams from the Iberian area to Central, Nordic and Eastern Europe in the early Middle Ages". In: M.G. Marques & D.M. Metcalf (eds), *Problems of Medieval Coinage in the Iberian Area* (Santarém 1988), pp. 255–268.

Moesgaard, J.C., "Stray Finds of Carolingian Coins in Upper Normandy,

France". In: I. Leimus (ed.), *Studia Numismatica, festschrift Arkadi Molvõgin 65* (Tallinn 1995), pp. 87–102.
— "Coin hoard, 64, Henouville, Seine-Maritime, France". *Numismatic Chronicle* (1997).
— "Eksporten af normanniske mønter til Østersøområdet i vikingetiden". *Nordisk Numismatisk Unions Medlemsblad* 4 (2000), pp. 84–86.
Morrison, K.F. & H. Grunthal, *Carolingian Coinage* (New York 1967).
Nissen-Jaubert, A., "Betragtninger over Camp de Péran". *Hikuin* 14 (1988), pp. 233–240.
North, J.J., *English Hammered Coinage*, vol. 1. 3rd ed. (London 1994).
Pagan, H.E., "The imitative Louis the Pious solidus from Southampton and finds of other related coins in the British Isles". In: P. Andrews (ed.), *The coins and pottery from Hamwic* (Southampton 1988), pp. 71–72.
Pol, A., "Münzfunde und Fundmünzen der Jahrtausendwende in den Niederlanden". In: B. Kluge (ed.), *Fernhandel und Geldwirtschaft* (Sigmaringen 1993), pp. 189–204.
Skaare, K., "Die karolingischen Münzfunden in Skandinavien und der Schatzfund von Hon". *Hamburger Beiträge zur Numismatik* 20 (1966), pp. 393–408.
— *Coins and coinage in Viking-Age Norway* (Oslo 1976).
Smart, V., "The moneyers of St. Edmund". *Hikuin* 11 (1985), pp. 83–90.
Stoess, C., "Die Münzen". In: E. Wamers (ed.), *Die Frühmitttelalterlichen Lesefunde aus der Löhrstrasse (Baustelle Hilton II) in Mainz* (Mainz 1994), pp. 177–189.
Völkers, H.H., *Karolingische Münzfunde der Frühzeit* (Göttingen 1965).
Weiller, R., *La circulation monétaire et les trouvailles numismatiques du Moyen Age et des temps modernes au pays de Luxembourg*, I–III (Luxembourg 1975, 1989, 1996).
Wiechmann, R., *Edelmetalldepots der Wikingerzeit in Schleswig-Holstein* (Neumünster 1996).

Jens Christian Moesgaard

Joël Callais

A Thor's hammer found in Normandy

Recorded finds of Viking artefacts are extremely rare in Upper Normandy. The state of research has been conveniently summarised by Patrick Périn (Périn 1990). It is a pleasure to be able to add a new item to his list. This object is almost unpublished, as it has only been mentioned once in the relevant literature (Renaud 2000: 80).

It is a so-called Thor's hammer, which is a small pendant, shaped as a hammer, representing the hammer of the Viking God Thor. It is made of almost pure silver (see below) and weighs 4.74 g. Its maximum length is 38 mm, and its maximum width is 22.5 mm. It seems to have been moulded and then hammered. Its surface is decorated with an irregular pattern of holes made by pressing circular and square poincons into the metal. The loop is made by hammering the metal and then twisting it into a swan-like shape. It is a typical Viking artefact, except for the unusual form of the loop which, nevertheless, is paralleled by an iron Thor's hammer found at the cemetery at Hesselbjerg, Parish of Randlev, Jutland (Andersen & Klindt-Jensen 1971: 31 & note 1), and which is dated to the Viking Age.

Figs. 1–4. Thor's hammer found in Normandy. Length 38 mm. Width 22.5 mm.

This small piece of jewellery was found on the slope above the River Seine in the Bois de la Fontaine, a little east of the hamlet l'Anerie (Parish Saint-Pierre-de-Varengeville, dép. Seine-Maritime). The find spot is just below a Celtic hill-fort (Wheeler & Richardson 1957: 75–83), two metres from a path which goes down from the hill-fort to the riverbank. This path passes two minor ramparts that prolong the main double rampart on the plateau, and the Thor's hammer was found just west of these (i.e. inside the camp). The site has not yielded any other early medieval finds.

The metal of the Thor's hammer has been tested by the engineers of Sønderborg Teknikum (University of Southern Denmark). The metal composition was analysed by EDAX (electron activation) at four different spots on the surface:

	Iron	Silver	Copper
1	–	99.08%	0.92%
2	3.15%	96.08%	0.78%
2 without iron	–	99.19%	0.81%
3	–	99.50%	0.50%
4	2.83%	96.01%	1.16%
4 without iron	–	98.81%	1.19%

The spots for testing were selected at places without visible corrosion. Tests 2 and 4 nevertheless showed the presence of iron, which presumably comes from contamination from the environment. Therefore, the results for tests 2 and 4 when subtracting the iron are also indicated in the table. Generally speaking the metal composition of the surfaces that have suffered the effects of the production process and that of corrosion is not the same as the composition of the core, which is closer to the overall metal composition of the item. The figures obtained by the surface analysis, nevertheless, indicate a very high silver content.

Of course, the find of a Viking artefact in Normandy inevitably raises the question whether it is genuine or not. The Vikings are an integrated part of the present day popular picture of Normandy, and modern copies of the Viking artefacts made as practical jokes or as scientific fakes cannot be excluded. A popular Danish archaeological magazine, *Skalk*, which is read by some people in Normandy, has published an illustration of the Hesselbjerg

Joël Callais

Thor's hammer (1971, no. 3) and has sold silver copies of it (1979, special issue no. 2). Nevertheless, the general public in France is not familiar with the Thor's hammer and I have never seen Thor's hammers as souvenirs, etc., in Normandy. If it is a fake, it must have been made by a specialist. However, in my opinion, the high silver content, which is not a common feature today, is an argument in favour of the object being genuine. So is the very remote and inaccessible find spot. But, of course, none of these arguments are absolutely sure.

Note
I would like to thank Patrick Périn, Lizzi Thamdrup, Ulla Lund Hansen, Else Roesdahl, Jens Christian Moesgaard and Sønderborg Teknikum for help, information and useful comments. Anne Pedersen kindly drew my attention to the Thor's hammer from Hesselbjerg. The opinions expressed on the authenticity of the artefact are mine and do not in any way engage the above-mentioned persons. This paper was completed in 2000. It has not been updated.

Translation by Jens Christian Moesgaard.

References
Andersen, H.H. & O. Klindt-Jensen. "Hesselbjerg. En gravplads fra vikingetid". *KUML* (1970), 31–41.
Périn, P. "Les objets vikings du Musée des Antiquités de la Seine-Maritime, à Rouen". In: *Recueil d'études en hommage à Lucien Musset. Cahiers des Annales de Normandie* 23 (Caen 1990), pp. 161–188.
Renaud, J. *Les Vikings en France* (Rennes 2000).
Wheeler, M. & K.M. Richardson. *Hill-Forts of Northern France* (Oxford 1957).

Else Roesdahl

Viking art in European churches
(Cammin – Bamberg – Prague – León)

Introduction

Four unique Viking objects preserved in European treasuries have caused much speculation as to how and why they came there. They have been treated separately and seen either as booty, or presents to foreign visitors after the Viking Age, or as belonging to Scandinavian royalty living abroad. All these ideas were based on the concept that Viking art objects were held in low esteem in contemporary Europe, and that Scandinavian aristocracy and royalty at that time lived in some cultural isolation from their counterparts to the south and west. This article re-examines all four objects and presents a different interpretation, based on a different notion of the prestige of Danish royalty and of Viking art around the turn of the first millennium. The objects treated here are seen as examples of royal gifts, presented soon after they were made, in a similar context to many other objects (including caskets and swords) which travelled throughout Europe in the Middle Ages.

*

Four splendid Viking objects were for centuries preserved in European church treasuries. These are the Cammin (Kamień) casket, the Bamberg casket, the so-called St. Stephen's sword in Prague and a small box in León (in coastal Poland, Bavaria, the Czech Republic and northern Spain, respectively). All are made of antler or walrus ivory and are top-quality examples of the Mammen style; stylistically, therefore, they must have been produced in Scandinavia or by Scandinavian artists elsewhere at the end of the 10th century.[1] Three of these objects were published in Goldschmidt's ivory catalogue of 1918; the fourth was published in the 1926 volume on Romanesque ivories.[2] The León box was not internationally known until then and, because it appeared in a later volume, it was largely forgotten by Viking research until attention was again drawn to it in 1990.

In 1998 I published an article in the Festschrift for Michael Müller-

Fig. 1. The Cammin casket. Formerly in the cathedral of Kamień in coastal Pommerania, Poland. Now lost. Drawing Magnus Petersen. After Kornerup 1875, p. 25.

Wille[3] which, I believe for the first time, considered all four objects together and took into account their quality and fascinating provenances. All but the Cammin casket came from places outside usual spheres of Viking influence or contact. All were preserved in churches of distinction, linked to royalty or princes. All these churches are situated in places, which were, by the late 10th century, on the fringes of Christian Europe or in areas that had recently been converted. Hence, I interpreted them as examples of royal gifts to foreign contemporaries from a Scandinavian king newly converted to Christianity, Harald Bluetooth, or, possibly, his successor, Sven Forkbeard. Previously they had been interpreted as loot from foreign campaigns in Scandinavia in the Viking Age or later, or as 12th-century gifts to European visitors to Scandinavia. Here I would like to elaborate on my 1998 article and place these objects in a wider context. I shall start with some background and a description of each of them.

The Cammin casket, fig. 1, comes from the cathedral of Kamień

Else Roesdahl

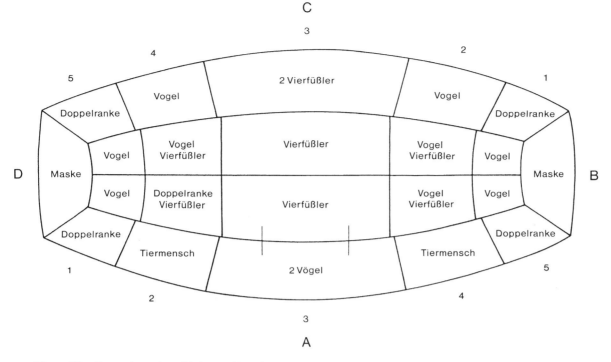

Fig. 2. The Cammin casket. Main motifs. After Muhl 1990, Abb. 20.

(Cammin) in coastal Poland. It was probably first recorded there in 1617. Lost during evacuation (destroyed or looted) at the end of World War II, it is known only from descriptions, pictures and casts. It was described in detail by Arnold Muhl, 1990.[4]

It was house-shaped, 69 cm long. Highly ornamented plates, probably of elk antler, were applied to its wooden frame by means of ornamented, gilt copper-alloy binding strips. It had six short legs, and on one of the long sides was a prominent lock-plate that engaged with hasps, hinged to a panel on the roof, which served as a lid. The casket contained relics said to be of St. Cordula (one of the 11,000 Virgins), but as her grave and bones were 'found' in the 13th century, this dedication must be secondary. Nothing in the ornament suggests a Christian meaning: rather it comprises large animals, birds, masks and other ornaments of the Mammen style, fig. 2.

Kamień is situated near the southern shore of the Baltic Sea and close to Wolin, a town of great importance during the Viking Age and for a century after. It was a pagan region, a meeting place of many religions. Kamień is also in a part of the world in which there is plenty of archaeological evidence of Scandinavian presence and of connections with Scandinavia in the Viking Age and later. As an example one might cite the marriage alliances of two Danish kings: Harald Bluetooth married an Obodrite princess and Sven Forkbeard married a Polish princess. A different example of such contact is provided by a hoard of high-quality gold jewellery found in 1872–74 on the small island of Hiddensee, off the island of Rügen, not so far from Wolin. This hoard has often been interpreted as a royal gift connected with Harald Bluetooth, or as a hoard lost by him. This theory is tied into a tradition recorded by Adam of Bremen that Harald Bluetooth fled to Wolin (Jumme) after being defeated in the rebellion led by his son Sven Forkbeard in about 987; he was well received in Wolin, but died shortly after from his wounds. Wolin became the seat of the bishops of Pomerania in 1140, but after repeated attacks on Wolin by Danes, the See was moved to Usedom and later, between 1174 and 1180, further to Kamień. In the 12th century Kamień became the seat of the princes of Pomerania, and when the bishopric was transferred to this town Prince Casimir founded a cathedral.[5]

Various suggestions have been made about the early history of the casket. For example, that the casket was carved by a Scandinavian artist who lived in the Wolin area, or that it was presented by Archbishop Asser of Lund (died 1137) to Bishop Otto of Bamberg on the latter's diplomatic embassy to Lund around 1128. In the latter case it would have been a very old object. It has even been suggested that the casket was looted by Slavs from Kungahälla, near present Gothenburg, in 1135.[6] I, however, would suggest that it was a gift from Harald Bluetooth to a Slav prince, and that it was first kept in the princely treasury and later presented to Wolin or Kamień Cathedral.

The Bamberg casket, fig. 3, probably comes from St. Stephen's church in Bamberg, Bavaria, where it seems to be the reliquary casket first recorded in 1608. It was, probably, sold during the secularisation in 1805 and was in private ownership until the Bayerisches Nationalmuseum in Munich bought it in 1860. It was discussed in detail by Muhl 1990 together with the Cammin casket.[7]

It measures approximately 26 × 26 cm. Its oak frame is decorated with highly ornamented panels of walrus ivory clasped by ornamented, gilt, copper-alloy mounts which are nailed to the wooden base. In the middle of

Else Roesdahl

the lid there is a rock crystal. The original lock was in the lid (the lock and keyhole in the side were added later). The ornament corresponds to that of the Cammin casket and has no hint of Christian significance, fig. 4.

The Bamberg casket is traditionally known as "Kunigunde's box", and has often been related to Knut the Great's daughter Gunhild/Kunigunde. She married the future Emperor Henry III in 1036 and died shortly after, in 1038/39. But the association with Kunigunde (which was also the name of the wife of the Emperor Henry II) is probably due to confusion with another casket (now lost) from the treasury of the Bamberg cathedral.[8]

Fig. 3. The Bamberg casket. Length 26 cm. Formerly probably in St. Stephen's church in Bamberg. Now in the Bayerisches Nationalmuseum, München. Photo: Bayerisches Nationalmuseum München.

Viking art in European churches (Cammin – Bamberg – Prague – León)

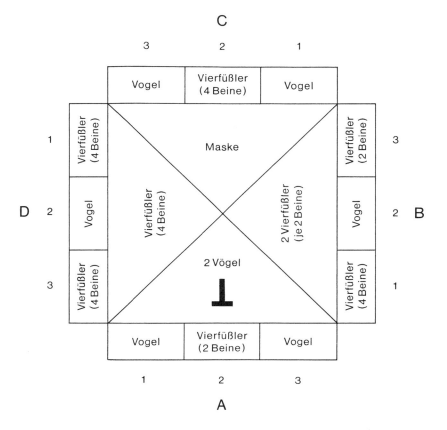

Fig. 4. The Bamberg casket. Main motifs. After Muhl 1990, Abb. 2.

Bamberg, however, was near the eastern frontier of the Empire and close to pagan territory. It was the favourite residence of the Emperor Henry II (1002–24) and his wife Kunigunde (died 1031/33); indeed, the town was presented to Kunigunde in 997. At Henry's request Bamberg was elevated to bishopric in 1007. Construction of the church that later became a cathedral was started by Henry II in 1002. St. Stephen's church, however, was founded by the first bishop between 1007 and 1009 with support from the royal couple. Rich gifts, including books that had been in the possession of Henry's predecessors, were bestowed on institutions in this town.[9] The casket may have been among these gifts.

St. Stephen's sword, figs. 5–6, is part of the treasury of the St. Veits' (Vitus) Cathedral in the Prague Castle. It is first mentioned in connection

Fig. 5. Both sides of the hilt of the so-called St. Stephen's sword in St. Vitus' Cathedral in Prague Castle. Length of guard 9.2 cm. Photo: David M. Wilson.

with the cathedral in 1355 as *gladius beati Stephani regis Ungarorum*. There is no recent publication of the sword, which is not easily accessible.

The sword is of Jan Petersen's type T, dated to the second half of the 10th or the first half of the 11th century. Its shortened blade (the sword is

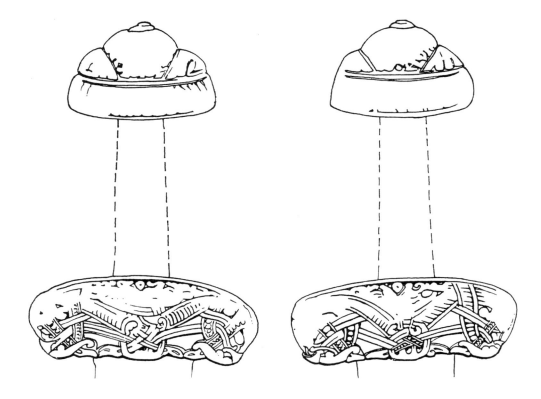

Fig. 6. Both sides of the hilt of the so-called St. Stephen's sword in Prague. After Košnar 1991.

only 75 cm long, having been ground to a new tip) has an etched Ulfberht inscription. The material of pommel and guard (length 9.2 cm) is ivory and the grip is bound with silver wire. The once elaborate carving of the guard (its two sides are almost identical) is much worn. It is generally agreed that it was decorated in the Mammen style, which also implies that the ivory of the pommel and guard probably derives from a walrus (elephant ivory was hardly used in Scandinavia at that time).[10]

Chronologically, the sword may indeed be related to Saint Stephen, first king of Hungary (997–1038), who converted his country to Christianity and was crowned in 1001. His relics were enshrined in 1083. Goldschmidt and others have suggested that the sword came to Prague in 1304 with the Hungarian royal insignia and remained there when the others were re-

Figs. 7–8. The box in San Isodoro, León. Height 4.5 cm. Photo: Jan Skamby Madsen 1990.

turned; they are now in Budapest. Alternatively, the sword's history may be different and, perhaps, related to the fact that the Bohemians were converted to Christianity around 900 or in the first half of the 10th century, and that Prague became a bishopric in 972/73. St. Veits' became a cathedral and, being situated in the Castle, was near the seat of secular power.[11] There is no reason, therefore, why the sword could not have come directly to Prague from Scandinavia and remained there. The much worn guard and pommel suggest that it had been in use for some time.

The León box, figs. 7–8, is part of the treasury of the collegiate church of San Isodoro in León. Largely forgotten until recently by those who study the Viking Age, it has not been the subject of any modern publication.[12] Indeed, many of the previously published photos show it upside-down.

Viking art in European churches (Cammin – Bamberg – Prague – León)

It is 4.5 cm high, 3.3 cm in diameter and cylindrical with a protruding 'ear' at the top, which is also masked by a hinged lid (the hinge itself is not original). The cylinder is made of antler (not, as is sometimes said, of ivory or bone), the ear being carved from one of its tines. The lid and the base are of gilt-copper alloy. The whole piece, including the lid and the base, is richly ornamented in openwork in the Mammen style. The quality of the carving is very fine. Goldschmidt records that it contained a relic; today it is empty.[13]

This box has no known parallel in Scandinavia and it seems probable that it was specially made as a Christian pyx – to hold the host – or, rather, as a reliquary – to hold a relic, either of which could be seen through the openwork walls or the lid. In form and decoration it is clearly related to Scandinavia. The 6 cm high bone cylinder found in a grave in Årnes (region of Møre og Romsdal, Norway) is similar in form (save that it has no ear) and in style,[14] while the ornament of the metal base of the León box is reminiscent of Scandinavian disc brooches of the 10th century. The ornament of the lid resembles the decoration of some of the smaller panels of the Cammin casket.[15] There is nothing of Christian significance in the ornament: the main motive is a bird, similar, for example, to those on the mounts of the Cammin and Bamberg caskets and on the Hiddensee pendants.

It has been suggested that the box came to León from the Isle of Man, where fine stone crosses, decorated in the Mammen style, still survive. Or that its appearance might be due to Viking incursions in northern Spain. Or that it was presented to San Isodoro together with other gifts by King Fernando I (1037–1065) and his Queen.[16] The latter proposition does not seems unlikely. León is indeed situated on a cultural crossroad in an area of great interest to Christians and known to Scandinavians in the late 10th century. The town was the capital or royal residence of the kingdom of León, and it is not far from Santiago de Compostela, where the cult of St. James had been celebrated since the early 9th century, originally on a local basis. León is indeed on the pilgrims' road to Santiago. Pilgrims from north of the Pyrenees are first recorded at the shrine of St. James in the early 10th-century, although pilgrimage to this place does not seem to have developed into a mass phenomenon before the 11th or 12th century. Furthermore, Santiago and León were situated in the Christian part of the Iberian Peninsula, but close to the border of what was in the late 10th century Muslim territory.

Else Roesdahl

León was stormed by Almanzor in 987, and Santiago was destroyed by him in 997, while Vikings had plundered Santiago and occupied the region in the years 968–71. The church of San Isodoro was founded in 1063 by King Fernando I to commemorate victories over the Moors, and the relics of San Isodoro were transferred to the church from Seville. Fernando had united the realms of León and Castile in 1037, and San Isodoro became a burial church for his dynasty. It was, then, a church of great distinction and closely associated with royalty.[17] The box may well have been in royal possession for some time before it came to San Isodoro, and it may first have been in another royal chapel or church in the region.

These four high-quality objects were, then, preserved in churches that were either founded by, or had close connections with, princes or kings, and the Prague sword (according to a 14th-century source) is associated by name with a royal saint. Three of them are likely to have been produced for secular use (the Cammin and Bamberg caskets with their locks and the Prague sword); none bears recognisable Christian iconography or even a Christian symbol. It seems reasonable to suggest that they left Scandinavia soon after their production as diplomatic gifts, presented by a king to kings or princes in various parts of Europe. They were rare and exotic objects which would have been worth treasuring. It is farfetched to assume that they (or some of them) left Scandinavia much later, during the 12th century, for example.

It is now widely acknowledged that Scandinavian Viking kings had many peaceful contacts with their European counterparts, and that diplomatic and other connections probably became more important towards the end of the 10th century, when these four objects were made, in a period when Danish kings were newly converted Christians. Chronologically and historically Harald Bluetooth would seem to have been the most likely donor. Indeed, the Mammen style may have been developed at his court (the grandest example of the style is the rune-stone which he had carved at Jelling).[18] The ornament on the two caskets and on the León box is closely related to the art of Harald's period; indeed, some of the pictures may symbolise power. Another possible Danish donor could have been his successor, Sven Forkbeard. There is every reason to believe that these two Danish kings exchanged gifts with German kings and emperors (which may account for the Bamberg casket) and with Slav princes (which may relate to the Cammin casket), while many suggestions can be made as to why Harald or Sven would present a sword to a Hungarian or Czech king and a reliquary to a king or royal shrine in Christian Spain.

Indeed, fine swords were a usual gift between princes – for example, in 873 the Danish king Halfdan's diplomatic envoy presented the German king Louis with a gold-hilted sword.[19] However, gifts for princes might comprise anything from swords to fine rings, books or even ships. In 1040, for example, Earl Godwin presented the Danish-English king Harthacnut with a splendid ship manned with eighty lavishly armed warriors.[20] As for the caskets, they may have been elaborate containers for gifts that now are gone – comparable to a relic in the León box (assuming it was a reliquary), and generally comparable to the 8th-century Anglo-Saxon 'Franks casket' from Auzon, in Auvergne. According to a recent theory it could have been an elaborate container for a precious book, now lost, made for a king or a prince and presented to a Frankish church.[21]

Finally, I would like to see these four Viking objects in a wider context. They are certainly not the only elaborate objects to travel far in medieval Europe and to have an unknown story. Among such objects are many caskets, including the 'Franks casket', the Anglo-Saxon 8th-century casket from Gandersheim, Saxony,[22] and the so-called Ranvaik's casket, which was produced in Ireland or Scotland in the 8th century and perhaps looted by Vikings. This casket was, according to a runic inscription, owned by a woman called Ranvaik about the year 1000, and it contained silk-wrapped relics when it came to the Danish Royal Collections from a Norwegian church some time before 1737. It is possible that the function of this casket changed from clerical to secular use and then back again to clerical as a reliquary. It is now a much travelled museum piece.[23] And in the 12th and 13th centuries large numbers of reliquaries of varying quality were produced in Limoges, in the south of France, and spread all over Europe.[24]

Among high quality objects found far away from their place of origin are a number of Scandinavian articles made of the same type of material as the Viking Age objects discussed here. These include the Lewis chessmen, made of walrus ivory in the late 12th century in Scandinavia (probably in the Trondheim region) and found on the Isle of Lewis in the Hebrides; they are usually explained as trade goods lost on the way to Dublin.[25] A walrus ivory horn from the 13th century, which once probably was in Sainte-Chapelle, Paris, was carved in Norway and has a Scandinavian runic inscription; it is suggested that it was presented by the Norwegian king Magnus Lagabøter to

Else Roesdahl

the French king Philippe III in exchange for a piece of the Crown of Thorns. It is now in the Bargello Museum in Florence.[26] Another large Scandinavian horn of finely carved walrus ivory is known from Europe. According to the coat of arms it was produced for King Christian I of Denmark (died 1481) and Queen Dorothea. It is suggested that it was brought as a gift during the Queen's pilgrimage to Rome in 1488 or, possibly, during the King's journey to Italy in 1474. The horn is said to come from Nola in southern Italy. In 1870 it was in Schlossmuseum Gotha in Thuringia, but, like the Cammin casket, it disappeared during World War II and is now known only from descriptions, good pictures and a cast.[27]

It is interesting that royal gift-exchange has for a long time been a common explanation of the presence of high quality medieval objects of Scandinavian origin in southern Europe, while quite different explanations were used for comparable objects from the Viking Age. The concept behind this is, no doubt, that art objects decorated in Viking styles would have been held in low esteem in 'civilised' contemporary Europe and that Scandinavian royalty ('barbarian Viking kings') was culturally isolated from royalty to the south and west. This concept is surely wrong – especially with regard to Christian kings.

Postscript

This article was finished in 2000. Since then an elegantly carved 11th-century Tau-crozier head has been excavated at the Veszprémvölgy convent in Hungary; it probably comes from a destroyed grave and is said to be made of walrus ivory. It is carved in the Scandinavian Ringerike style, or possibly in the Hiberno-Norse version of this style. It is not known how it came to Hungary. See A. Fülöp & A. Koppány, "A crosier from the territory of the Veszprémvölgy convent", *Acta Archaeologica Academiae Scientiarum Hungaricae* LV (2004). The León box will be re-published by the present author in the proceedings of the Fifteenth Viking Congress, Cork 2005 (forthcoming).

A close parallel to the Bamberg casket with regard to shape, size and type of lock was found in 2004–06 in a woman's grave at Haldum in Jutland, Denmark. It was of wood with iron mountings. See Jens Jeppesen & Marianne Schwartz, "Fornemt skrin – I en kvindegrav fra vikingetid". *Kuml* 2007 (English summary).

Notes

1 The Mammen style is treated in detail by Fuglesang 1991; the Prague sword and the León box are, however, not included in her list of examples of the style. Regarding the Mammen style, see also Wilson & Klindt-Jensen 1966: 95–133; Wilson 1995: 115–141.
2 Goldschmidt 1918: nos. 189, 191, 192; idem 1926: no. 298.
3 Roesdahl 1998.
4 Muhl 1990: 296 ff.; see also Goldschmidt 1918: no. 192; Wilson & Klindt-Jensen 1966: 126; Fuglesang 1991: no. 15 et passim, with refs.
5 Muhl 1990: 325 f. with refs.; see also Adam of Bremen, II: 17–18; Swiechowski 1983: 29, 251–253; Filipowiak 1988; *Lexikon des Mittelalters* V, 1991: 'Kammin'; Filipowiak & Gundlach 1992. On the Hiddensee hoard see Paulsen 1936; Roesdahl & Wilson (eds) 1992: cat. no. 265.
6 Summarised and discussed by Muhl 1990: 323–329.
7 Muhl 1990: 243 ff., discussion of the material 259 ff.; see also Goldschmidt 1918: no. 189; Wilson & Klindt-Jensen 1966: 124–126; Fuglesang 1991: no. 14 et passim, with refs.
8 Muhl 1990: 244–246.
9 *Lexikon des Mittelalters* I, 1977: 'Bamberg'; Mayer 1988: 8 f., 234 ff.
10 Goldschmidt 1918: no. 191; Paulsen 1933: 52–58 (on the material of the guard he says "aus Elfenbein, vielleicht nur aus Bein"); Wilson 1965: 50; Wilson & Klindt-Jensen 1966: 127, 132; Müller-Wille 1970: 74, 83 no. 2 with refs.; Košnar 1991: 62 ff., 82–84. On the use of walrus ivory see Roesdahl 1995. It has occasionally been thought that the so-called St. Wenzel's helmet, which is also in the treasury of St. Vitus' Cathedral, bears some relation to Viking art; cf. for example Košnar 1991: 83 with refs. I am grateful to David M. Wilson for discussing the sword with me and providing photos of the hilt.
11 Goldschmidt 1918: no. 191; *Lexikon des Mittelalters* VII, 1994: 'Prag'.
12 See, however, my Postscript to this article.
13 Goldschmidt 1926: no. 298 (with two photos); Gaborit-Chopin 1978: 91 and cat. no. 84 (with a different photo; she describes it as a pyx); Morales 1991: 46 et passim (with many photos); Vinayo 1998: 46 (with a colour photo; the material is described as reindeer antler; if this identification is correct, the box may have been produced in Norway, but see below); *Lexikon des Mittelalters* VII, 1994: 'Pyxis'; cf. Backhouse, Turner & Webster (eds) 1984: cat. no. 116. The box was re-discovered for Viking archaeology by Jan Skamby Madsen during a visit to Spain in 1990 and published with pictures in Danish newspapers, including *Politiken*, on 13 December 1990, with an identification of the material as red deer antler by the Zoological Museum, Copenhagen (based on good photographs). A colour photo is published in Skamby Madsen 1992: 18. The first publication of the box in 1925 is mentioned by Morales 1991: 46. This date probably explains why the box was included in Goldschmidt's vol. IV (1926) and not in vol. II (1918), which has the related objects. I am grateful to Jan Skamby Madsen for providing photos for this article.
14 Wilson & Klindt-Jensen 1966: 128, pl. XLV:b-e; Graham-Campbell 1980: no. 495; cf. also the bone cylinder with incised ornament ibid. no. 500; Fuglesang 1991: no. 17.
15 For example Jansson 1984: 60 f. with fig. 8:2 (type I); Muhl 1990: Taf. 22.
16 Skamby Madsen 1992: 19. On Manx crosses see Wilson & Klindt-Jensen 1966: 108 ff.; Wilson 1983; Kermode 1994 (1907). The most extensive discussion of the box's possible history is in Morales 1991: 46 f.
17 On the history of Santiago de Compostela, León and San Isodoro see, for example, also *Lexikon des Mittelalters* V, 1991: 'León'; VII, 1994: 'Santiago de Compostela'; Vinayo 1972; idem 1998. On Viking adventures in the region, see Fabricius 1897: 130 ff.
18 Op. cit. in note 1.
19 *Quellen zur Karolingischen Reichsgeschichte* III (Annals of Fulda).
20 Whitelock (ed.) 1955: 291 (Florence of Worcester).
21 Webster 1999.
22 Webster & Blackhouse (ed.) 1991: cat. no. 138.
23 Youngs (ed.) 1989: cat. no. 131.
24 O'Neill et al. (ed.) 1996.
25 Stratford 1997.
26 Blindheim 1972: cat. no. 5; Gaborit-Chopin 1978: cat. no. 120.
27 Hildebrand 1873; Hildebrand 1884–1898: 494, 511, figs. 104–106, 388 f., 404; *Riddarlek och tornerspel* 1992: kat. nr. 20; Tegnér 1992.

Else Roesdahl

References

Adam of Bremen: see *History of the Archbishops of Hamburg-Bremen*.

Backhouse, Janet, D.H. Turner & Leslie Webster (eds), *The Golden Age of Anglo-Saxon Art* (London 1984).

Blindheim, Martin, *Middelalderkunst fra Norge i andre Lande / Norwegian Medieval Art Abroad* (Oslo 1992).

Fabricius, Adam K., "Normannertogene til den spanske Halvø". *Aarbøger for Nordisk Oldkyndighed og Historie* (1897).

Filipowiak, Wladyslaw, "Handel und Handelsplätze an der Ostseeküste Westpommerns". In: *Oldenburg – Wolin – Stara Ladoga – Novgorod – Kiev. Berichte der Römisch-Germanischen Kommision* 60 (Mainz 1988).

Filipowiak, Wladyslaw & Heinz Gundlach, *Wolin Vineta* (Rostock 1992).

Fuglesang, Signe, "The axehead from Mammen and the Mammen style". In: M. Iversen (ed.), *Mammen. Grav, kunst og samfund i vikingetid* (Højbjerg 1991).

Gaborit-Chopin, Danielle, *Elfenbeinkunst im Mittelalter* (Berlin 1978; translation of *Ivories du Moyen Age*, Fribourg 1978).

Goldschmidt, Adolph, *Die Elfenbeinskulpturen* II *aus der Zeit der karolingischen und sächsischen Kaiser* VIII.–XI. *Jahrhundert* (Berlin 1918; reprint Berlin 1970).

— *Die Elfenbeinskulpturen* IV *aus der romanischen Zeit* XI.–XIII. *Jahrhundert* (Berlin 1926; reprint Berlin 1975).

Graham-Campbell, James, *Viking Artefacts. A Select Catalogue* (London 1980).

Hildebrand, Hans, "Drottning Dorotheas jakthorn". *Vitterhetsakademiens Månadsblad* (1873).

— *Sveriges medeltid* 2 (Stockholm, 1884–98; reprint Stockholm 1983).

History of the Archbishops of Hamburg-Bremen by Adam of Bremen, trans. F.J. Tschan (New York 1959).

Jansson, Ingmar, "Kleine Rundspangen". In: G. Arwidsson (ed.), *Birka* II:1. *Systematische Analysen der Gräberfunde* (Stockholm 1984).

Jørgensen, J.H., in *Politiken*, 2nd section, p. 3 (13 December 1990).

Kermode, P.M.C., *Manx Crosses. With an introduction by David M. Wilson* (Angus 1994; first published London 1907).

Kornerup, J., *Kongehøiene i Jellinge* (Copenhagen 1875).

Košnar, Lubomír, "Ke vztahum mezi vikinskym a západoslovanskym prostregím. – Zum den Beziehungen zwischen dem wikingischen und westslawischen Milieu". *Praehistorica* XVIII (Varia Archaeologica 5) (1991).

Lexikon des Mittelalters vol. I, 1977 (Bamberg); vol. V, 1991 (Kammin; León); vol. VII, 1994 (Prag; Pyxis; Santiago de Compostela) (Munich and Zurich).

Mayer, Heinrich, *Bamberg als Kunststadt* (Bamberg 1955; reprint Bamberg 1988).

Morales, Eduardo Romero, "Arte vikingo in Espana". *Revista de arqueologia*, vol. XII, no. 12 (May 1991).

Muhl, Arnold, "Der Bamberger und der Camminer Schrein. Zwei im Mammenstil verzierte Prunkkästchen der Wikingerzeit". *Offa* 47 (1990).

Müller-Wille, Michael, "Ein neues Ulfberth-Schwert aus Hamburg". *Offa* 27 (1970).

O'Neill, John P. et al (eds). *Enamels of Limoges 1100–1350* (New York 1996).

Paulsen, Peter, "Wikingerfunde aus Ungarn", *Archaeologia Hungarica* XII (1933).

— *Der Goldschatz von Hiddensee* (Leipzig 1936).

Quellen zur Karolingischen Reichsgeschichte. III. *Jahrbücher von Fulda. Regino Chronik. Nother Taten Karls*, rev. R. Bau. Freiherr vom Stein-Gedächtnisausgabe (Darmstadt 1960).

Riddarlek och tornerspel (Stockholm 1992).

Roesdahl, Else, *Hvalrostand, elfenben og nordboerne i Grønland*. C.C.Rafn-forelæsning nr. 10 (Odense 1995; French version, "L'ivoire de morse et les colonies norroises du Groenland". *Proxima Thulé* 3 [1998]).

— "Cammin – Bamberg – Prague – León. Four Scandinavian *Objects d'Art* in Europe". In: A. Wesse (ed.), *Studien zur Archäeologie des Ostseeraumes. Festschrift für Michael Müller-Wille* (Neumünster 1988).

Roesdahl, Else & David M. Wilson (eds), *From Viking to Crusader. Scandinavia and Europe 800–1200* (Copenhagen 1992; New York 1992).

Skamby Madsen, Jan, *Les Vikings Danois* (Copenhagen 1992).

Stratford, Neil, *The Lewis Chessmen and the Enigma of the Hoard* (London 1997).

Swiechowski, Zygmunt, *Romanesque Art in Poland* (Warsaw 1983).

Tegnér, Göran, "Drottning Dorotheas jakthorn". *Historiska Nyheter* 52 (1992).

Vinayo, Antonio Gonzáles, *L'Ancien Royaume de León Roman* (Zodiaque 1972).

Vinayo, Antonio Gonzáles, *Colegiata de San Isidoro* (León 1998).

Webster, Leslie, "The iconographic programme of the Franks casket". In: J. Hawkes & S. Mills (eds), *Northumbria's Golden Age* (Stroud 1999).

Webster, Leslie & Janet Blackhouse (eds), *The Making of England. Anglo-Saxon Art and Culture AD 600–900* (London 1991).

Whitelock, Dorothy (ed.), *English Historical Documents*, vol. I, *c. 500–1042* (London 1955; reprint 1961 and later).

Wilson, David M., "Some neglected Anglo-Saxon swords". *Medieval Archaeology* IX (1965).

— "The art of the Manx crosses of the Viking Age". In: C. Fell et al. (eds), *The Viking Age in the Isle of Man* (London 1983).
— *Vikingatidans konst*. Signums svenska konsthistoria 2 (Lund 1995).
Wilson, David M. & Ole Klindt-Jensen, *Viking Art* (London 1966; reprint 1980).
Youngs, Susan (ed.), *'The Work of Angels'. Masterpieces of Celtic Metalwork 6th–9th centuries AD* (London 1989).

Contributors

JAN BILL is Professor in the Department of Archaeology at the Museum of Cultural History, Oslo University, Norway.

JOËL CALLAIS is a water supply engineer (retired) and an amateur archaeologist, Duclair, Upper Normandy.

IBEN SKIBSTED KLÆSØE is Assistant Professor of Archaeology at the Saxo Institute, University of Copenhagen, Denmark.

EGGE KNOL is Curator of Archaeology and History at the Groninger Museum, Groningen, The Netherlands.

LAURENT MAZET-HARHOFF is an Archaeologist and a Coordinator for the Prehistoric Areas Historical-Archaeological Experimental Centre, Lejre, Denmark.

JENS CHRISTIAN MOESGAARD is Assistant Keeper at the Royal Collection of Coins and Medals, National Museum, Copenhagen, Denmark.

ELSE ROESDAHL is Professor in the Department of Medieval and Renaissance Archaeology at Aarhus University, Denmark.

W.J.H. VERWERS is a Research Archaeologist (now retired) at what was formerly the Rijksdienst voor het Oudheidkundig Bodemonderzoek, Amersfoort, The Netherlands.